Also by Ga

Occult Ex

The Pract

Magical Images and the Magical Imagination

Merlin and the Grail Tradition

Pythoness: the Life and Work of Margaret Lumley Brown

Esoteric Training in Everyday Life

In this Series:

The Magical World of J.R.R. Tolkien

The Magical World of C.S. Lewis

The Magical World of Charles Williams

The Magical World of Owen Barfield

The Magical World of

J.R.R. TOLKIEN

Gareth Knight

Sun Chalice

Published by

Sun Chalice Books

PO Box 5355, Oceanside. CA 92052 USA

sunchalice@earthlink.net

Library of Congress Control Number: **2001092878**

ISBN 1-928754-08-2

Cover and book design by Nicholas Whitehead

Table of Contents

1.
IN THE BEGINNING

J.R.R.Tolkien caught the imagination of a generation with his trilogy, *The Lord of the Rings,* with massive sales and the development of what practically amounted to a complete sub-culture of enthusiasts. This led later to the publication of the source material for it all, in *The Silmarillion* and other works carefully researched and recovered from old manuscript material by his son. Tolkien did no less than construct his own mythology and body of legend from a vast store of Anglo-Saxon and other early literature gathered from his own reading, the apparent neo-paganism nonetheless entirely compatible with his deep Christian faith.

From this body of private myth and legend he drew stories of many different kinds, a creation cycle, fall from paradisal innocence, ancient sagas of forgotten races and peoples human and non-human, including stories of lovers and heroes. He had begun to write such stories at an early age and by the age of eighteen had conceived the idea of writing a complete cycle. His prime source of wonder was in fairy stories, and in the ancient concept of the word, perhaps better rendered as *faery*, which implies that realm of the imagination that is considerably more "magical" or mythopoeic than arch tales of sentimental fancy.

Through early manhood he kept all this as a private occupation until, in 1929, after a lively discussion on the gods and giants of Asgard, he showed some of it to his Oxford University colleague, C.S.Lewis, who responded with enthusiasm and encouragement. For some time Lewis was his only audience.

Indeed, in a letter Tolkien later confided to a friend: "only from him did I ever get the idea that my stuff could be more than a private hobby."

Since his schooldays Tolkien had also been captivated by the power of language, and he developed a particular love for Early English and Old Icelandic. This enthusiasm he took over into his professional academic life, insisting that "language" should be the basis for teaching literature, and advocating that more attention should be paid to teaching ancient literature as a subject worthy of study in its own right, rather than as a short introduction to modern literature courses, consisting merely of "gobbets" from anthologies. He excited some backstairs amusement in considering even Shakespeare and Spenser as "modern" writers. Shortly after his arrival at Oxford he formed a little club called the "Coalbiters," to popularise the reading of Old Icelandic.

His first published work in this genre was however a children's story called *The Hobbit.* This commenced in a typical "magical" way in recording the rising of images in the imagination. At the time Tolkien's mind had been half-engaged on the boring task of marking school examination papers, when, on a blank sheet of paper he was suddenly impelled to scrawl the phrase: "In a hole in the ground there lived a hobbit."

This was the beginning of the children's story that eventually expanded into *The Lord of the Rings*. Prior to this incident, he had no idea what a hobbit was, and indeed had to write the subsequent story in order to find out. In so doing he was sowing the seeds of a literary phenomenon that affected the consciousness of a whole generation. *The Lord of the Rings* became a best seller and was, in a sense, an example of a group initiation.

If we seek a reason for this it may well be found in the depth to which Tolkien plumbed the imagination in his mythopoeic quest, for both *The Hobbit* and *The Lord of the Rings* were but a small fragment of a vast mythological scheme, the core of which was not published until after his death, as *The Silmarillion*.

This contains a creation story, in which Ilúvatar, the One God, the Father of All, creates the angels and the angelic worlds before the Earth ever was, followed by the fall through pride of one of their number and the consequences that this had upon the paradisal world and later upon the world of elves and men and hobbits and all the other creatures, with the resultant battles against evil which reflect the condition of the world to this day.

It will be helpful if we pay some attention to these early happenings, for they are the mainspring from which the rest of the action develops, with very far reaching consequences. Without consideration of *The Silmarillion,* much of the action of *The Lord of the Rings* and *The Hobbit* cannot be understood.

2.
THE AINULINDALÉ

The primal creation story appears at the beginning of *The Silmarillion* as a short book entitled *Ainulindalé* or *The Music of the Ainur*. It commences with the basic statement that in the beginning was One God, Eru, the One, who in Arda was called Ilúvatar, and he made first the Ainur, or Holy Ones, that were the offspring of his thought, and they were with him before anything else was made.

Arda is the realm of the Earth, and Ilúvatar simply means, in the Elven language "Father of All." The Holy Ones, or offspring of his thought, could be called archangels, or gods, or even Elohim, in the language of men, although Ainur in the Elvish tongue.

The first creation was not that of the physical world but of a system of higher worlds; what might be called archetypal patterns. This was no mathematical abstraction but a beautiful living world that can only be comprehended in terms of music, of harmony, or what we might call The Great Music.

Since Ilúvatar had kindled within each of the Ainur a spark of his own divine creative fire, they each had their own creative contribution to make. They were not mere organ stops or keys destined to produce a particular note when impressed by the divine player. Nor were they even orchestral performers reading off a score under direction of a conductor. Rather were they contributors to a great free collective improvisation, each one adding an individually composed melody to the general harmony and counterpoint. This was the original "harmony of the spheres" before the starry systems were produced to spin and dance to its measure.

As in any improvised music, this presupposes that all are agreed upon a common theme, or ground bass. But it came into the heart of one of the Ainur, called Melkor, to introduce his own variations that were out of key with the basic divine theme. Thus an element of discord was introduced into the heavenly music.

At first Ilúvatar, the Supreme Being, countered this discord by introducing a new theme to counterbalance and harmonise the discordant elements, making the "wrong" notes resolve in a right progression, as indeed is within the powers of any accomplished musician skilled in improvisation. However, the contending discords of Melkor rose up even to oppose this second theme, whereupon Ilúvatar introduced a third theme, to make all harmonious again, but yet again Melkor's pursuit of his own inharmonious themes resulted in all the music being brought to a close in one great last chord.

In the silence that followed Ilúvatar confronted all the Holy Ones, and as a means of instruction into the principles of divine creation, said that he would now show them the results of their music making. He directed their attention into the Void, and there, visible to their sight, was a whole universe of starry spheres. These had been created by their music.

In the contemplation of the results of their music making they saw strands that were not made by them, but which had been introduced by Ilúvatar to counterbalance the discords of Melkor. Of these, the third great theme was seen to be the creation of the races of Elves and of Men, who were thenceforth collectively known as the Children of Ilúvatar, the special creation of God himself.

It is important to realise that Elves and Men are of one original stock; one branch simply awakening before the other, so that the Elves are sometimes called the Firstborn, and Mankind are called the Followers. In more esoteric parlance they might be referred to as sub-races of one root race of spiritual beings. Or, as Tolkien himself specifically stated, Elves are early Men, not yet fallen entirely from the paradisal condition, hence their great beauty and supreme skill in arts and crafts. The Holy Ones also see the place chosen for the habitation of Elves and Men, in the midst of the sea of stars. This is Arda, or the Earth.

All this is but a visioning or foreshadowing of that which is about to be brought into being in the Void. This ground of creation is like that which is found in a doctrine of the Holy Qabalah known as the *tsim-tsum*, which is the void made by the omnipresent God within himself, to give space in which the creation can exist. We find therefore in Tolkien's story a fleshing out of Qabalistic doctrines, probably not known to him consciously but intuitively conceived through his great imaginative powers.

It then falls upon the Ainur to leave the "Timeless Halls" and enter into the Void themselves to help to bring about the creation that they have fore-sung in heaven. The chief part in this is taken by four of them, named Manwé, Aulé, Ulmo and Melkor. To Manwé belongs all the creation that pertains to what was anciently known as the Element of Air. To Aulé belongs all that pertains to the realms of Elemental Earth. And to Ulmo the Element of Water. In this context the term Element means far more than the hundred or so atomic structures known by this term in modern chemistry. In the ancient magical sense that Tolkien intends, they each comprise a whole mode of physical, psychic and spiritual expression, that manifests in the physical state as solid, liquid and gas.

Melkor was originally ranked the highest of the Ainur and he presides over the Element of Fire, which is a created expression and counterpart of the Divine Imperishable Flame of Ilúvatar. But his persistent pursuit of his own idiosyncratic themes gives him a role that constantly acts against the constructive efforts of the other Ainur. Thus the Earth in its primeval history goes through many tumults of a volcanic nature. There are periods when the Ainur walk a near-perfect Earth, a kind of Earthly Paradise of angelic beings, a Golden Age. But this is periodically overthrown by the acts of Melkor, who works with Fire in a distorted or degraded way. Yet being responsible for this most powerful, transformative, holiest of Elements, it may well be that his burden, and his temptation, is greater than that of the others.

To the lesser eyes of Elves and Men, the Children of Ilúvatar, the works of Melkor appear wholly evil. However, in another great imaginative insight Tolkien describes Elves and Men as bearers of the Third Theme. And this, by extension, is the *true* expression in the form worlds of the Cosmic Fire. In other words, Elves and Men are graced with Divine Sparks that, if truly developed in accordance with their holy destiny, may put the world to rights. However, it is to be expected that Melkor will be diametrically opposed to this, being the bearer of the form of Fire that they are set to overcome. Hence the perpetual confrontation of Melkor and all his works with the race of Elves and Men. Thus is the cosmic stage set in the pages of the Ainulindalé of the original "fall" from heavenly unity by the Holy Ones, and the formation of the archetypal divine plane for the destiny of the Earth.

3.
THE VALEQUENTA

The short book that follows in *The Silmarillion,* called *Valequenta*, is an account of these archangelic beings according to the traditions handed down by the Elves, who call them Valar, or the Powers of Arda (or Earth). Men, it is stated, often called them gods; and among men their names are manifold. However, in the *Valequenta* we are given a complete and balanced system of these powers, as opposed to the fragmented and confused pantheons of the gods of the various races of men.

In the Elven tradition the principal powers are fourteen in number, seven lords and seven ladies, who had "put on the raiment of Earth and descended into it." They are as follows.

MANWÉ, Lord of the Breath of Arda, who besides being the ruler of all, and closest in love and understanding to Ilúvatar, is particularly associated with the powers of the Element of Air.

VARDA, his consort, the Lady of the Stars, whom the elves hold in particular devotion, under the name of Elbereth. Of indescribable beauty, she shares a palatial abode with Manwé among the very highest mountains of Earth.

ULMO has no consort, but is a mighty Lord of the Waters, which includes not only the seas and oceans but every lake, river, rill and fountain. Therefore his spirit is to be found throughout the whole world, wherever there is life-giving moisture. Next to Manwé he is the greatest of the Valar.

AULÉ is Lord of all the substances of the Earth, next in order of power, and a great smith and master craftsman. He is particularly honoured by the elves as a teacher and master of these arts, and especially for his gem and crystal lore. In a number of respects the fallen Melkor resembles him in thought and powers, hence the mistaken notion that sometimes occurs among men that the underworld is a place of evil. It is simply that the tumults and disorders of Melkor are aimed more generally at the realm and substance of Aulé.

YAVANNA, his consort, is the Giver of Fruits, who loves all growing things, and is thus the Mistress of Nature. She is often seen as a tall woman robed in green, although she can appear in many guises, and in particular in the form of a great tree, stretching from the depths of the Earth up to the Sun. The elves call her Kementári, Queen of the Earth.

NAMO, who is also called Mandos, after his dwelling, is known as Keeper of the Houses of the Dead. He is also keeper of the records of the lives and destinies of all. In short he is a kind of recording angel.

VAIRÉ, his consort, is the Weaver, who has a great tapestry upon which she embroiders all that has happened in the worlds of Time. In more eastern esoteric terms Nama would therefore be reckoned as a Lord of Karma, or Destiny, and Vairé as the keeper of the akashic records.

IMRO is another Valar lord who is more generally known by the name of his abode, which is Lórien. This is a beautiful paradisal garden from which all can gain rest and refreshment.

ESTÉ, his consort, is the Healer, and Bringer of Refreshment to all who seek repose and the easing of burdens upon her island of trees that is situated on a lake in the Summerlands of Lórien.

NIENNA is a great lady of the Valar and sister of Namo and Imro, who mourns every pain and sorrow that is ever suffered in the world as a result of the works of Melkor. In this she is the teacher of compassion to all who listen to her, and of steadfast endurance in faith and hope.

TULKAS, called the Valiant, is a great warrior, wrestler and strong man, who came to Earth especially to aid in the early battles against the disruptive works of Melkor. He is no great source of wisdom or counsel but is a staunch and loyal friend in times of need or danger.

NESSA, his consort, is fleet footed, and the lover of dancing and of running deer.

OROMÉ is a great lover of the things of Earth, and is known as Lord of the Forests. He is sometimes seen as a great hunter of monsters and foul creatures. He rides a swift white or silver horse, and the sound of his horn is like the breaking of dawn or the flash of lightning in the darkness.

VÁNA, his consort, is the Ever-young, who is like a Maiden of Spring and the Dawn. Flowers open at her approach and birds begin to sing.

It would be possible to draw parallels with various gods and goddesses from various pantheons of the gods of men. There are, in this game of correspondences, no hard and fast rules, but the evaluation of similarities is an educative exercise in comparative mythology. It helps one to appreciate the different approaches of different races at various times to the one underlying reality of the universal powers; and to judge how they either lack completeness or emphasise one aspect at the expense of another. This acts as a kind of macrocosmic mirror to any racial soul. It may also help one to tap into one's own intuitive knowledge of the true and the good, and the pattern of its expression.

Above all, in the Tolkien schema, we have a clear indication of the true relation between the various creative levels. That is, the Valar, or the angels, or the gods, are themselves created beings. Thus although they are capable of sub-creation, they should not be worshipped as substitutes for Ilúvatar. They are greater and more powerful than men, as trees, or elephants, or power stations, are greater, each in their way, but this does not mean that men should bow the knee to them.

This applies whether we are thinking in terms of the gods of the pagans, or the choirs of angels of Judaeo-Christian tradition, or the creative hierarchies of occult speculation. The Valar serve as a model for each. It is important to keep this in mind as the scenario becomes more complex with the advent of other orders of being, which come into the burgeoning Earth from the cosmic realms.

In the Valaquenta these are described as helpers of the Valar, and are generically known as the Maiar. Of these, some of the more important are:

ILMARÉ, the handmaid of Varda, the lady of the stars;

EÓNWÉ, the herald and standard bearer of Manwé, the lord of the Valar;

OSSÉ, master of the seas that wash the shores of the lands of men and elves, under the great water lord Ulmo;

UINEN, lady of the seas, and consort of Ossé, who might be considered queen of the mermaids, sirens and other sea creatures, who is also the friend of mariners in that she can quell a storm.

Thus we have a certain distinction of reverence and attitude towards these different beings. Certainly the elven sailors may have called upon Uinen, the lady of the sea, to help them in distress, and paid her all due reverence, as in latter days human travellers might have called upon the blessing and intercession of St. Christopher. The Roman Catholic church has of course taken pains to make a clear distinction between worship of God (called *latria*) and reverence to saints, angelic or human (called *dulia*).

This becomes of particular importance when we come to consider the role and status of the "Enemies" or the forces of evil in the scheme of things. The one originally known as Melkor ("He who arises in Might" in the Elven tradition) would in human annals be referred to as Lucifer, "the light bearer." However, the elves, who suffered grievously from his pride, malice and deception, renamed him Morgoth, "the Dark Enemy of the World." In the words of the *Valequenta*: "He began with the desire of Light, but when he could not possess it for himself alone, he descended through fire and wrath into a great burning, down into Darkness."

He is one who was originally of the Valar and of at least equal power and importance to Manwé. This is why it is important to be clear about their cosmic standing. If we deny the supremacy of Ilúvatar, the One God, the Creator of All, then by the same token we render ourselves prey to the evil powers of Morgoth, which we have inadvertently raised. At the same time we fall into the trap of Dualism, acknowledging equal power to evil and to good, instead of seeing evil as a mere temporal aberration that must come to naught in the end because it has no noumenal reality in terms of the Eternal.

As there are servants of the Valar, so are there servants of Morgoth, in their equivalent ranks, an infernal distorted reflection of the hierarchy of the heavens. Thus Sauron was in the beginning a server of the great Valar Aulé, but turned to evil and the service of Morgoth, and became known to the elves as Gorthaur the Cruel.

Thus the stage is set for the main book, the *Quenta Silmarillion,* which is the unfolding of the history of the world as recorded by the elves.

However, in the beginning, before the appearance of elves and men, the Valar created a paradisal kingdom on Earth. These are the primeval times before there is even Sun or Moon as we know them. They dwell on an island in the midst of a great lake, which is lit by two wondrous lamps that they have fashioned. However, this golden age is marred and overthrown by Melkor, who has built his own rival abode, a stronghold deep within the Earth.

The effect upon Earth of Melkor's actions is the blight and disease of vegetation, the development of monstrous and carniverous beasts, and eventually the overthrow and breaking of the great lights. All the primal creation is thus destroyed, and henceforth the Valar are no longer to be seen on the physical Earth itself (or Middle-Earth, as it is called).

They withdraw to the very "westernmost rim" of the world, where they raise Holy Mountains inaccessible to any but themselves. And so their earthly paradise is recreated, not on Earth itself, but on a remote outpost of Earth known only to a few, and dreamed of later by mankind as wondrous lands in the far west, the Hesperides.

However, from this vantage point, the Valar can observe all that happens on Earth. Here in this guarded realm they build a great city, called Valmar of the Bells. And before it, on a green mound, they create a meeting place for their high councils. And upon the mound are two wonderful trees, one of green and silver, and the other of green and gold. They give light to all, as had the great lamps in the previous age, before they were overthrown by Melkor. The two trees also shine alternately, and this is the very beginning and measure of recorded time.

In Middle-Earth itself, abandoned by the Holy Ones, and called by them the Outer Lands, all is in constant twilight, lit only by the distant stars, as there is still no Sun or Moon. Melkor still lives in his deep underground stronghold, and Ulmo remains present in all the waters, and dwells in the Outer Ocean which surrounds the whole Earth. These Holy Ones with a deep love for the things of Middle-Earth are also still to be found wandering therein from time to time: Oromé, the Lord of the Woods, and Yavanna, the Lady of Nature. And ministering spirits of Manwé fly out like eagles and hawks from his mountain fastness at the end of the world to report whatever goes on. And so they await what they recall as the "third theme" of the Great Music of Heaven, the coming of the Children of Ilúvatar to redeem the world that has fallen through the fault of angels.

But in the depths of the Earth Aulé cannot contain himself in patience waiting for their coming, so he creates a race of beings himself, to whom he can teach his arts and crafts. This sub-creation is later to be known as the race of Dwarves. They were allowed by the compassion of Ilúvatar to live, despite their irregular creation, particularly as Aulé had acted in good faith and humility. However, they are put into a species of hibernation until such time as the elves and men are established upon the Earth, in accordance with the divine plan. Theirs is the spirit of technology which has come to pass only in recent times in the race of men. But even in those distant times of early creation Yavanna foresaw that this would eventually bring about a conflict and a suffering to the natural world. "They will love first the things made by their own hands..." she says, "They will delve into the earth, and the things that grow and live upon the earth they will not heed. Many a tree shall feel the bite of their iron without pity."

As a consequence of her concern, it is revealed that there shall be a power within the forests that will exert its wrath upon those who abuse the trees. It would appear that the high-tech ecological crisis that faces the modern world was here forewarned and foreshadowed. There is always a relevance to contemporary human problems in whatever Tolkien wrote in mythological vein.

This is not because it is, or was intended to be, any form of allegory or social comment. It is more likely that when the imagination is deliberately set to work with mythological themes and motives, a deeper truth emerges which often has a bearing on current concerns and spiritual well-being. This is its magical ambience in terms of the functioning of the secondary imagination. What appears at first as mere subjective fantasy turns out to be an act of sub-creation that surprises and instructs even its inventor. In such a way was Aulé surprised by the independence from himself of the dwarf kingdom that he created from his own imagination.

This particular subcreation of Aulé occurred at a period of enforced idleness awaiting the coming of a new phase in creation. This kind of situation is referred to in some of the annals of occult cosmology, for instance in Dion Fortune's *Cosmic Doctrine*, where it is called "epigenesis", resulting in complexities, not always of happy consequence, caused by "creations of the created" while awaiting a new phase to come to pass in the evolutionary scheme of things. A major exemplification, it might be said, of the proverb that the devil finds work for idle hands!

However, the time comes, far back in the annals of Earthly time, for the awakening of the Elves. This occurs, by tradition, by the waters of a great lake, under the stars, when Orion and Sirius were first seen in the night sky. There is as yet still no Sun or Moon, and the configuration of the Earth is very different from how it is today.

The absence of Sun and Moon should prove no stumbling block on account of its apparent absurdity in terms of modern astrophysics. This is simply a consequence of a limitation in the scope of our imaginative faculties, that are currently dominated by an assumption that mind and the physical universe are separate and discrete, or that mind is simply a by-product of the physical. If all is realised to originate primarily in the sphere of mind then a totally different cosmology can result, and what Blake called Newton's " dark satanic mills" will then be realised to be but a temporary mental prison house, and greater truth seen to reside in mythopoeic perspectives.

In the beginning, the Elven children of Ilúvatar were stronger, fairer and more glorious than they were later to become. They were, by tradition, first encountered by the Hunter of the Valar, Oromé, in his journeying through the woods of Middle-Earth as Lord of the Forests. In recognition of their great beauty he called them "the people of the stars" – the Quendi, or Eldar. The cause of their gradual loss of power, glory and beauty was the continued machinations of Melkor, whose works, it was their divinely appointed destiny (along with Men) to overcome.

Some of the elves were actually ensnared, captured and enslaved by Melkor, and in the course of time, through a process of planned genetic degradation in his underground caverns, became a fearsome race of servants in later ages, known as Orcs. This was considered by some to be the most vile act ever done by Melkor. The Orcs themselves loathed their master deep within their hearts, for their service was based on fear and their ancestry from a source of deeply ingrained misery.

It was this kind of activity that brought about a further war of the Holy Ones with Melkor. Unable to watch this corruption and tyranny go further, by the counsel of Ilúvatar himself, the Valar swept from their secluded place and smote Melkor and all his works. So great was this conflict that the very configuration of the Earth was changed. The Land of the Holy Ones also became more profoundly separated from the rest of the Earth by a Great Sea, the same that is described in many of the myths and legends of latterday men in terms of Eldorado or Hy Brasil or the Lands of the Blessed. Unhappily for future ages, not all the deepest caverns of Melkor's iniquity were discovered, scoured out and cleansed. But Melkor's main power base was destroyed and he himself taken in chains to the abode of the Holy Ones. Here he was imprisoned in the further reaches of the Halls of Mandos for long ages.

During this time the Holy Ones were concerned over the fate of the Elves, and after some debate decided that it was too dangerous for them to remain alone in the world, and so a place was found for them on the fringes of the Far West, in the pure lands the Holy Ones had made for themselves. From this decision, compassionate in intention but in effect unwise, came many of the ills that were later to afflict the world and the Elves. It was, after all, the destiny of the Children of Ilúvatar to dwell in the world and make it good. Insofar as the Holy Ones themselves had failed to do this it was perhaps natural that they should assume it to be beyond the powers of the Children of Ilúvatar. However, in this they were doubting the will and wisdom of Ilúvatar, and diverting his Children from their true destiny. Most of the Elves heeded the summons to go to dwell in the beautiful lands of the West, although a number went with reluctance, and some not at all. Perhaps heeding the deep dim call of their own sense of destiny, they rejected the apparently more attractive life to be found in a protected paradisal zone beyond the bounds of Middle Earth. Thus came about what is recorded in their annals as the First Sundering of the Elves.

4.
SAGAS OF THE ELVEN PEOPLES

The rest of *The Silmarillion* is for the most part concerned with the sagas and various happenings of heroes and heroines of different branches of the Elven peoples. The first division of the Elves (or the Quendi, in their own language) was between the Eldar and the Avari.

The Eldar were the elves who undertook the great journey into the West. Their name – "the People of the Stars" – was given to them by Oromé.

The Avari (meaning the Unwilling) did not undertake the journey out of Middle Earth. They were also called the Sylvan or Woodland Elves.

The Eldar can again be divided into three branches for the purpose of the later annals, the Vanyar, the Noldor and the Teleri.

The Vanyar, or Fair Elves, went to the West and dwelt there ever after in peace and harmony under the protection of the Holy Ones.

The Noldor, or Deep Elves (deep in the sense of possessing great knowledge and not necessarily profound wisdom), through the subtle corrupting influence of Melkor brought strife even into the land of the Holy Ones. It was these elves who created the Silmarils, the great jewels from which much trouble was later to come.

The Teleri were the last, and largest, host of elves to make the great journey to the West. Hence their name, which means "Latecomers" or "Hindmost", although they preferred to call themselves the Lindar, or "Singers."

There were, however, two branches of the Teleri who failed to complete the westward journey. These were the Sindar and the Nandor.

The Sindar, or Grey Elves, remained on the westernmost coast of Middle Earth itself, without actually crossing the Great Sea to the Land of the Holy Ones.

The Nandor left the westward march even before this, and did not come within reach of the Great Sea. Their name means "those who turned back." A branch of them were later called the Laiquendi, or Green Elves, from the leaf-green colour of their raiment. They dwelt in the elm woods.

And over all we have a fundamental division of the Elves into the Calaquendi and the Moriquendi.

The Calaquendi, or "Elves of Light" are sometimes called the High Elves. They consist of the Vanyar, the Noldor and those Teleri who made the journey to Aman, "the Blessed Realm free from evil" in the Far West beyond the Great Sea. They are called the Elves of Light because they knew the light of the Two Trees that stood at the council mound of the Holy Ones.

The Moriquendi, or "Elves of Darkness" are so called not because they were evil but because they never saw the light of the two paradisal Trees.

We have therefore a process of the spreading of various Elven peoples throughout the regions of the world, stretching from the withdrawn "Blessed Realm" through to the tree dwellers of Middle Earth itself. Between these two extremes were the intermediate realms, with a number becoming Sea Elves, or skilful mariners on the Great Sea. The Great Sea is of course an inner condition in occult terms, and represents the division between the higher ethers of the paradisal Blessed Realm and the conditions of the dense physical world itself, Middle Earth.

Things were later to be complicated by the return to Middle Earth of the Noldor after a sojourn in the Blessed Realms. This is the gist of the bulk of *The Silmarillion* and it would serve little purpose to outline all of it in detail here. However, in broad terms the events are important in view of the consequences that they brought about. This revolves principally around the fashioning of the Silmarils, and their subsequent fate.

In the course of ages Melkor was eventually released from his imprisonment in the Halls of Mandos. He abased himself and sought pardon of Manwé, the Head of the Valar. Manwé, being free from all thoughts of evil, took Melkor's repentance at face value and granted him freedom, although others of the Valar were uneasy about it, in particular the more worldly Ulmo and Tulkas. Having been granted his freedom Melkor set about subtly corrupting the Elves under guise of helping them. He had a concealed but deep seated hatred of them, and associated them with his previous downfall.

The Noldoran Elves delighted in crafts and skills and the fashioning of things of great beauty. A supreme aim that the brightest of their number conceived was the fashioning of three great jewels that would contain the blended light of the Two Trees. That is, marvellous and near-miraculous gem-stones, containing the light of paradise. Such indeed was their exquisite beauty that they became the cause of terrible strife, for they proved to be temptations beyond the moral strength of those who fashioned them. This of course revealed the very worst in the fallen Melkor, who desired their power and beauty for himself. Truly did Mandos, the Lord of Destiny, foretell that the fate of the very Earth itself lay locked within these artefacts of supernal beauty.

The high princes of the Noldor treasured these jewels with an increasing jealousy and avarice until, under the influence of the whispered insinuations of Melkor, they began to distrust even the Holy Ones, suspecting that they might be envious of their great possessions. Thus there came about an actual rebellion of Elves against the Valar. As a consequence Melkor's evil designs were unmasked, and he fled from the land of the Holy Ones.

Féanor, the leader of the elven revolt, was banished from the City of Bells, with his seven sons. They still remained in the Realm of the Blessed however, but retired to a mountain fastness, where they kept the Silmarils and their other treasures, including newly forged weapons, in iron chambers.

It was soon after this that Melkor made an unexpected strike from his hidden places in Middle Earth and destroyed the paradisal Trees. This meant that their original light was now contained only in the Silmarils. These were captured and carried off by Melkor, who was now called by Féanor, the creator of the Silmarils, Morgoth, the Black Foe of the World. The Silmarils remained in Morgoth's power, although their purity was such that they burned anyone evil or impure who touched them. Nothing loth, Morgoth had them set in his iron crown.

Féanor, in the meantime, embittered beyond reason, blamed his loss entirely upon the Holy Ones, and led the Noldor back to Middle Earth. This was a journey of much tribulation, in the course of which, distrust and internecine fighting broke out between the different branches of the Elves. Féanor also swore with his sons a great oath, vowing vengeance even to "the ends of the World" on any "Valar, Demon, Elf or Man as yet unborn, or any creature great or small, good or evil, that time should bring forth unto the end of days, whoso should hold or take or keep a Silmaril from their possession." As a consequence of this implacable oath much further strife was to ensue. The initial seeds of distrust sown by Melkor had borne a strange, long lasting and bitter fruit.

It is at this point that the Sun and Moon were created, as a source of light for Middle Earth, that had been so far illuminated by starlight alone. These luminaries were placed close to the Earth so as to hinder the works of Melkor. They were also, in their way, memorials of the two paradisal Trees. Each was put under the guidance of one of the Maiar, an angelic spirit in the service of the Holy Ones. As a consequence, Melkor, or Morgoth, withdrew himself deepeer into the depths of Middle Earth. And so the paradisal light that dwelt in the Silmarils was now deep in the heart of the Earth, in Morgoth's iron crown. There are obvious parallels in all of this with legends of the fallen Lucifer and the Holy Grail being formed from a jewel in his crown.

Valinor, the land of the Holy Ones in the Far West, was now made even more inaccessible to Middle Earth. The Great Sea now held a barricade of enchanted islands to cast bewilderment upon any wandering mariner in these strange waters. In this there are further parallels with the man made myths of the Great Sea to the West, from the adventures of the star hero Perseus to the strange sea beyond the Forest of Broceliande in Charles Williams' Arthurian poems. With the coming of the Sun we move into the period when time can be reckoned in years as we now know them. And it is with the first rising of the Sun that the younger Children of Ilúvatar first appear, that is, the human race. Henceforth the annals treat of men as well as elves, although for the most part the two races, or sub-races, do not mix, despite the fact that they are close enough for the occasional mixed marriage, with resulting children.

5.
THE FOUR GREAT AGES

The latter part of *The Silmarillion,* together with *The Hobbit* and *The Lord of the Rings*, encompass four great ages before the recorded historical period of modern man.

The First Age commences with the creation of the Sun and Moon and the beginnings of humankind. It comprises the time of the long War of the Jewels as recounted in the *Quenta Silmarillion,* which ends with the Silmarils being won back from the crown of Morgoth. One is cast into the bosom of the Earth, another into the depths of the Sea, and the third taken into the Heavens, where it can still be seen, as the star of Eárendil, that men know as the Morning and Evening Star, or the planet Venus.

The Second Age, which is summarised in another section of *The Silmarillion* sees most of the Elves returned to the West, although for the most part not to dwell in Valinor again but in a lonely island within sight of it, called Eresséa. It is at this time that Sauron, originally of Valar rank, and a follower of Morgoth, begins to corrupt the world of men and of such Elves as remain in Middle-Earth. The latter who take pride in being superior to men, ordinary wood elves, and dwarves, strive to maintain remote places of ancient beauty untouched by time. One example of such is Rivendell or Imladris that is described in *The Lord of the Rings*. Sauron is able to subvert these fears of change toward aims of power, making an independent earthly paradise the equal of Valinor. With the help of the dwarves, the elves of one of these conclaves, Eregion at the foot of the Misty Mountains, succeed in making Rings of Power magically capable of slowing up the processes of decay. At the same time Sauron constructs a great Ruling Ring that will be capable of controlling all the others, as well as investing them with certain magical powers, such as invisibility.

The Elves, realising what is happening, try to destroy many of the rings, although three of them, particularly brilliant and powerful ones, they hide. A war results and Sauron obtains possession of many of the rings, giving them to those who were avaricious or ambitious enough to accept them not realising or not caring that they were the means to their corruption and the enslavement of their peoples.

From this is derived the ancient rhyme that provides the background to the action in *The Hobbit* and *The Lord of the Rings.*

Three Rings for the Elven-Kings under the sky,
Seven for the Dwarf-lords in their halls of stone,
Nine for Mortal Men doomed to die,
One for the Dark Lord on his dark throne
In the Land of Mordor where the shadows lie.

Sauron is helped, by these means also to corrupt the world of men who, as a reward for their aid the wars that end the First Age inhabit a great island in the Western Sea called Númenor, that is closely equivalent to the esoteric tradition of the lost continent of Atlantis, and is eventually destroyed through its own corruption and sinks beneath the waves. Considerable geophysical changes result from this, and the configuration of the Earth as we know it begins to take shape. (Thus the seas beneath which Atlantis sank, if it is to be identified with Númenor, were not the same as what is now called the Atlantic Ocean. Indeed the

Great Sea of these ancient times was halfway to Paradise, somewhere on the astral ethers.)

The Second Age is therefore the subject of two great annals, one telling the largely Elven story of The Rings of Power, and the other more concerned with the race of Men in The Downfall of Númenor. It ends however with a great alliance of Elves and Men that overcomes Sauron, and the One Ring is cut from his hand. His power departs and his spirit flees into the shadows but the evil power of the Ring still exerts itself in quarrels between the allies over its ownership. The one who takes it is however drowned in the Great River and the Ring lost.

The Third Age is the one in which the stories of The Hobbit and *The Lord of the Rings* take place, which account for only a very small period of time in the whole of The Silmarillion, whose initial roots indeed rest in eternity.

After a period of comparative calm evil begins to rise again. Sauron's monsters or slaves of the rings who were not wholly destroyed reappear. The Dark Tower and the evil land of Mordor remains, even if empty, with its borders carefully guarded. The Elves still retain some of their hidden places in Middle-Earth, maintained by the appointed guardians of their three Rings which have been preserved. Men have become the dominant race and gradually the old memories of Númenor and Sauron fade.

There is also the appearance of a lowly simple and unpretentious race of beings known as Hobbits, and in the end it is they rather than Elves or Men who finally achieve the rediscovery of the One Ring and its eventual destruction. Bilbo Baggins recovers it from the Gollum in *The Hobbit* when on a quest for dragon gold, apparently by accident (although whether it is the residual evil will of the Ring itself or the overriding will of Ilúvatar, or a combination of the two, is a matter for conjecture). This leads in *The Lord of the Rings* to the great mission that falls upon Frodo

Baggins and his friends to achieve its final destruction.

With the destruction of the Ring the Ring-bearers are translated to Valinor in the Land of the Holy Ones, the last of the elven ships departs from this world, and the Fourth Age, commencing with the earliest history of the world as we know it, begins.

6.
TOLKIEN'S MYTHOLOGY AND LANGUAGE

What are we to make of all this? As a daily newspaper asked on the publication of *The Silmarillion*: "How, given little over half a century of work, did one man become the creative equivalent of a people?"

The answer lies in the magical powers of the human imagination. Whether Tolkien realised it or not, and he probably consciously did not, he was using his mind in a very magical way. To begin with, there was his deep emotional response to the myths and legends that had meant so much to him in childhood, even to the extent of adding to them by making up his own stories based upon them. This is the way that the myths and legends were created in the first place. It is not an uncommon trait in many imaginative children; the difference is that Tolkien carried it through into his adult life.

Another factor was his continued allegiance to a mythology with which he had direct links both by land and by blood. Although there is a certain modern reluctance, because of racialist abuse, to take too much cognisance of the importance of place of birth or of ancestral blood lines, they are factors that do have a power beyond the rational, rooted deep within the instincts. These instincts are quite natural, and certainly not to be considered evil or atavistic, for it is upon them that natural human life is based, from loyalty to loved ones and to family, to peer groups and work mates, and local or national pride. In Tolkien we have a clear example of how an imaginative writer, exploring the natural lines of his heritage and ancestry, can gain access to very powerful inspirational forces that will speak to others within whom that mutual chord resonates.

Tolkien set out quite deliberately to write and to renovate the fragmented mythology of his land and people. With this spiritual will grafted on to his natural emotional attraction to it, we have a powerful combination in the active working of what Coleridge called the secondary imagination. His spiritual will in this direction also had almost a sense of religious mission. His commitment to the task he set himself was beyond all reason. There is something almost inhuman in the writing of a personal saga over all those years as a solitary venture, with almost no outside encouragement. Admittedly the encouragement he did receive was of a warm and personal quality, first through his wife Edith, and then through his friend and colleague C.S.Lewis, and via him to that group of Oxford friends known as the Inklings, and finally through his children, particularly Christopher, who has become the editor of a vast store of hitherto unpublished work. Indeed the solitariness could be seen as one pole of a psychic battery that pushed him into deeper realms of his imagination. It was a pure dedication, pursued entirely for its own sake, quarrying whatever he might find, without thought of what some commercial public might wish to read.

This spiritual will was also enhanced because he firmly believed, not only in the power of the imagination, but in its *sanctity*. Whether or not directly influenced by Coleridge's celebrated views on the matter, or Blake's, he was firmly convinced that imaginative writing was a species of *sub-creation*, particularly in the realm of myth making and legend – that indeed spiritual truths could be revealed by it. He expounds his views on this to a large extent in his essay *On Fairy Stories*, first published as part of a festschrift in honour of Charles Williams, and later, for more general readership, in a small volume called *Tree and Leaf*.

Beyond this, he also went back to fundamental dynamics, to the creative power of language itself, in that the myths and legends of the Elves came after his construction of a language and orthography for them. Indeed, as he stated almost in some surprise, having worked out the language, the mythology almost wrote itself as a natural consequence.

There are very deep matters of the springs of creation here. One is struck by the resonance of the opening lines of the most mystical of all four gospels: "In the beginning was the Word...." And it is no matter of mere accident or whim that the original traditions of Qabalistic mysticism are based firmly on a detailed analysis of the actual words of Holy Writ. The very letters are accorded special meaning and numerological significance. The basic roots of the Hebrew language are investigated with pious intent, each word-stem being a triune powerhouse of three letters. That this has been abused and degraded by popular superstition does not detract from it in the slightest. It is an area that has been accorded very little serious attention by sympathetic exegesis of Gentile commentators, despite frequent raids on the Hebrew mystical tradition. A study of the Zohar or any other genuinely mystical Qabalistic text is an entry to a different world indeed from the piecemeal interpretations and elaborations of post-Renaissance Gentile Qabalists, from Pico della Mirandola to the Hermetic Order of the Golden Dawn.

Some intuitions of the importance of the power of language, or the word, have indeed appeared over ensuing centuries but in very experimental, fragmented and even debased form. Perhaps the best known is the so-called Angelic language of the Elizabethan magus Dr. John Dee that came about as the result of clairvoyant investigation with the medium Edward Kelley, which has continued to exercise a fascination in certain occult circles. The mechanics of this are that there is nothing like a private language or code to concentrate the mind, or to bind the loyalties of a small group, which of course will apply particularly to those who may seek to bridge the communication gap between outer and inner planes. In more mundane circles it accounts for the growth of slang and argot, not to mention professional jargon.

It is language too that is often a major fact of differentiation between one race or nation and another, and even provinces within a single nation. Even when a common language is shared there may also be a wide cultural division marked by dialect or accent, either between geographical districts, between town and country, or in social class. Tolkien's friend and fellow Inkling, Owen Barfield, also aroused considerable interest with *Poetic Diction*, an analysis of how language reveals historical changes in human perception and consciousness, a work much admired by Tolkien.

Tolkien was particularly well prepared for a fundamental approach to language in that he was an advanced student of philology. Indeed he had studied at the feet of an amazing self-taught genius who pioneered this comparatively new academic subject. This was Joseph Wright, who from humble beginnings as an illiterate Yorkshire mill hand, taught himself to read and write in his teens, and setting sail for Europe, walked to the University of Heidelberg and enrolled there. Here, and at other continental universities, he studied languages to such good effect that on his return to England he was appointed Deputy Professor of Comparative Philology at the University of Oxford, and Tolkien studied under him as an undergraduate.

It is perhaps no irrelevance to note the strong Germanic roots of the discipline of philology, and the part played in it by two gentlemen who became more widely remembered as collectors of folk and fairy stories – the Brothers Grimm. It is almost as if some deep spring of knowledge came bubbling up from a profound depth as far back as the mid-nineteenth century, to run through the Brothers Grimm, Joseph Wright and Tolkien, and to burst into full flood with the rejuvenated version of the mythology of north-west Europe that is found in *The Lord of the Rings* and *The Silmarillion*.

Tolkien's imagination therefore first began to work upon a language that Elves might have spoken, together with the history of its various derivatives. So much did he put into this that other hands have gone on to produce grammars and dictionaries of it, such as *An Introduction to Elvish* by Jim Allan; some enthusiasts even write and speak it.

Working from roots as deep as this, it is perhaps not surprising that when talking of his work, Tolkien seemed to regard it as a subject matter separate from his own invention. He would talk of it as if it were an independent and entirely real and objective academic discipline. We submit that this was no mere quirk of vanity or professorial eccentricity, but rather evidence that Tolkien realised, or at any rate suspected, that his imagination was reading off deeper levels of existence and experience that had an objective validity of their own.

There can hardly be any more deeply magical conception than this, though it is more generally referred to in esoteric circles as "reading the akashic records." That is, imaginative access to the record upon the subtle ethers of all that has ever happened. It is no more than has been claimed for the visions of Rudolf Steiner, Madame Blavatsky and various others, including the remarkable natural clairvoyant Edgar Cayce.

Following from this it should be no great surprise to find qualities in common between Tolkien's imaginative fiction and certain basic occult traditions. This is particularly so in regard to the traditions of the lost continent of Atlantis, so broadly similar to Tolkien's Númenor. It is indeed arguable that Tolkien's imagination penetrated even deeper than this, that his vision extended to even more remote periods, vaguely referred to in occult tradition as Lemuria and Hyperborea. In terms of *The Silmarillion*, these are the remote ages of the first coming of the Holy Ones, and of the Elves and Men, in conditions before there was a Sun or Moon as we know them. Back almost to a paradisal condition, with a proto-human race that could recall the conditions of the Golden Age, or Edenic Earthly Paradise, before the full consequences of the Fall. And in all of this, it might be remembered, there is nothing at variance with Tolkien's Christian orthodoxy.

7.
THEMES IN TOLKIEN'S WORK

Two things that we may learn from the works of Tolkien are, first the incredible power and range of the human imagination when it is set up, triggered and nurtured in the right way. Second, the more or less objective structuring of the product of the human imagination on mythopoeic themes when operating in this mode.

A currently popular way of looking at this phenomenon is in terms of analytical psychology, wherein it is assumed that the mythopeoic writer is tapping levels of the unconscious to reveal a basic structure perhaps determined by brain configuration. However, reduction to psychological and even physiological or neurological terms may be as much a blind alley in this direction as it is in the sphere of religious experience.

It may be more fruitful if we outline the broad themes that may be discovered in the imaginative work of Tolkien. Then, even if one should subscribe to a psychogical interpretation, it may be conceded that important affective images may be like significant dreams. These we disregard at our peril, for they are a means to bring us to address problems of attitude or behaviour of which we are not yet fully conscious. So whether the source of inspiration be psychic complexes, or tutelary spirits, or clairvoyant powers, the end result may be beneficially the same. Handsome is as handsome does, in this largely uncharted area.

What are the broad themes that we discover in the imaginative work of Tolkien?

Ultimately the universe came into being through harmony – a theme that is sympathetic to the ancient traditions of Pythagoras, and to the Orphic Mysteries, and in general traditions ever since. This is seen at a late stage in Shakespeare's reference to the music of the spheres and Dryden's *A Song for St. Cecilia's Day*, beginning "From harmony, from heavenly harmony, this universal frame began..." The musicologist Joscelyn Godwin has produced some interesting books elaborating upon and anthologising this trend.

To aid in the building of the multiplicity of levels of the worlds, the One Creative Source called into being spirits capable of a measure of sub-creativity in their own right, under the divine direction and permission. These man calls angels or archangels in the monotheistic tradition, or gods when at a polytheistic stage of perception. The Hebrew word *Elohim* in the first verse of Genesis forms an interesting subject for conjecture in that this name for God the creator has a plural ending. The subject of angels is somewhat neglected by the modern church, although it formed a strong tradition in the Byzantine church and in the West in scholastic times up to the Renaissance Platonists. This was based upon the sixth century Platonic writings, *The Celestial Hierarchies,* produced under the pseudonym of Dionysius the Areopogite.

Because of the free will that this endowed power of sub-creativity gave, some of the builders were tempted to follow ideas of their own rather than the overall harmonious Divine Plan. These traditions of the Fall go back to early Hebraic tradition and have their more recent expression in the great poetic work of Milton, wherein the theme of *Paradise Lost* is made rich with imagery. The same metaphysical dynamics, although with different imagery, are to be found in *The Silmarillion.* Both may be considered, each in their way, "to justify the ways of God to men." Although Milton may be conceded to be the greater poet, Tolkien would appear to have attained the laurels of the greater popular following.

A further type of cosmic being is created to counteract the consequences of the archangelic Fall, the pre-human "War in Heaven." These are the Children of Ilúvatar, in other words the human race, in its broadest sense, incorporating the "elven" element that is in effect an Edenic branch of human expression. Although inferior in terms of power to the godlike angelic builders, they are immersed in the physical world which the angels created and have to some extent abandoned. Here, with all its imperfections caused by the Fall, and taking on the burden of imperfection within themselves, they have, by some mysterious means known only to Ilúvatar, the ultimate creator, the means of bringing things finally to rights. Tolkien's sagas extend only to the Third Age. The great "third theme" of the Music of the Ainur would presumably have its apogee in the Incarnation of Ilúvatar in human form, in the middle of the Fourth Age.

The created Children of God of the "third theme" are what might be termed a "chosen race" in the broadest cosmological sense. They divide up into a number of forms of expression, not only in the various races of men, but also of the elves, and a form in the Third Age hitherto little known in the grand elven annals, known as Hobbits. They can all three be regarded as of one spiritual stock.

Elves might be regarded as men in a semi-paradisal condition, immortal, capable of passing to the heaven worlds of gods or angels, brilliantly creative, beautiful, courageous; in a certain sense an ideal form of men compared to current human types and conditions.

The races of men in the Tolkien stories are more like men as we understand the term today, but in keeping with the remote ages in which the stories are set, they have a certain chivalrous or romantic air.

Hobbits, whose origin is obscure, although seemingly

portrayed as a separate race, have been said by Tolkien to represent a particular condition of the human species, not in any allegorical sense but in the qualities that are central to their character. That is, a prosaic ordinariness that is basically parochial, conventional, even small-minded, but capable of immense loyalty, devotion, and – when pushed to it – heroism. It is, after all, Frodo Baggins who ultimately defeats the mighty powers of evil at the end of the Third Age, not the warrior riders of the human kings or the armies of the elves, nor even the magic of the Maiar Gandalf/Mithrandir. It has been suggested, and seems not far from the truth, that the Hobbits owe a large part of their character in Tolkien's mind to the troops from the shires he met in the trenches in the First World War.

The three aspects of the Children of Ilúvatar, the Third Theme of the great Cosmic Symphony, might therefore be summarised as, in essence:

pre-fall and immediately post-fall humankind;

Homeric man of the legendary prehistoric ages;

man of the modern post-heroic era.

There has been a "War in Heaven" which continues to have its effect upon Earth at various levels, and which flares up on a kind of cyclic basis. At a very early period this was seen when Melkor destroyed the great lamps that lit the primeval Earth. A later stage on the critical spiral was when he invaded and destroyed the Two Trees in Valinor. Later periods come with the various wars with the Elves, culminating in wresting the Silmarils from his possession. Finally, in *The Lord of the Rings,* the great evil power rises again to be once again frustrated by Frodo and the company that forms around him. By extension we have similar crises recurring in the historical ages of man of which the most recent was perhaps the rise and fall of Nazi Germany, and the underlying dangers of the nuclear age.

The recurrence of evil centres about the most holy of objects. This is perhaps because it is in these that real power and ultimate beauty lies. By the same token they can be the root of great corrupting temptation, causing the independently centred will to attempt to set itself apart from the supreme will, love and wisdom of the One Creator of All. These holy objects are represented in the Tolkien mythology as Silmarils, wonderful gems that contain the light of Paradise. Later on we have a similar dynamic in the Rings of Power, and in particular of the One Ring that is capable of ruling the others. These rings, forged by Noldoran smith-elves under the evil direction of Sauron, had a power of their own that was capable of corrupting and dominating their very owners. Much the same could be said of certain aspects of modern technology. And in the religious sphere, it is the most holy sacraments, and holy writ itself that, as history shows, become the centre of the most rabid dissension – of which Jerusalem itself might be cited as an example.

In the battle against evil upon Earth magical forces are also engaged. That is, there are those capable of perception of inner world conditions and wielding powers thereof. This does not give omnipotent power, as the crucial actions have to be performed on Earth itself in physical deeds and moral action. However, it does have an important background influence, rather like intelligence services or undercover operations in times of hot or cold war. Representatives of such, on the side of evil, are the Nazgúl, former men who have become slaves of the rings. These appear as the Black Riders in *The Lord of the Rings*. Upon the side of good is the magician Gandalf the Grey, who becomes by virtue of initiatory sacrifice Gandalf the White, and who is also known to the elves as Mithrandir. He is representative of the organisational powers behind the scenes of the Orders of White Magicians, as opposed to the Dark Orders represented by the corrupt magician Sauron.

The origin of the great magicians is obscure, rather as with the Celtic Merlin, or the Biblical Melchizedek. They appear to be half human figures, or perhaps angelic or daimonic beings who appear in human guise. The inner forces extend in serried ranks and types, through various types of nature being, to the angelic and archetypal realms of the Maiar and the Valar. Opposed to them are fallen inner beings such as Morgoth, Sauron and the men and elves and other beings that they have corrupted or sub-created. Evil however is ultimately an illusion, a by-product in the created world of deviant wills. Ultimately all will conform to the original harmony conceived by Ilúvatar the Father of All, the leader of the great archangelic choir. In the meantime redemptive acts in the created world have to be achieved as best they may by those who strive to align their will, and the basic note of their being, to the plan and symphonic theme of Ilúvatar.

The importance of Tolkien's work is that he weaves a background tapestry that, while it need not in all detail be taken literally as recorded fact, nonetheless has for its basic outline a structure of objective overall reality. Once we have the basic structure in place, we have a scaffolding of the secondary imagination, so to speak, and we are at liberty to flesh it out with details or sub-creations of our own. This may seem to take on a life of its own, as a consequence of the basic rightness of the overall pattern. Thus what, as words on a printed page, are like a valley of dry bones, can, with the spark of the magical imagination, take on vibrant life. This can in turn teach us a great deal more about ourselves, our planetary destiny, and our place in the cosmic scheme of things.

Something of this process occurs in all forms of legend and mythology, and so therefore also in stories that are based upon mythopeoic principles. However, much mythological material, by its very nature, has been lost in the vicissitudes of time, and its survival through literary record is distorted or incomplete. The contribution of Tolkien has provided a “unified field” of mythology, stretching from the very beginning of creation, through the countless ages of prehistory, until the formation of the Earth as we now know it. It seems unlikely in the extreme that he realised the implications of this from the magical point of view.

These are that, just as it is possible to form patterns of integration, or sequences of initiation, using the basic material of myth and legend, so may Tolkien’s mythopoeic creative work be used in the same fashion, as if it were “real” myth and legend. In Tolkien, in short, we have the provision of a “seamless robe” of mythopoeic truth that is capable of yet further extension and elaboration by those who are sufficiently in tune with it.

8.
EXTENDING THE MYTH

Here follows an example of how this kind of thing can be done. It may be regarded as a meditation sequence or an exercise in group visualisation, with or without appropriate formal actions and accompanying music. At first sight it may appear no different from any normal play or pageant but there is much more to it, if properly performed, than a spectacle. It is capable of expanding consciousness and inner perceptions and thus is a modern equivalent of an ancient Mystery drama.

This particular piece, entitled "The Voyage West", is reproduced by kind permission of Mrs. Vivienne O'Regan, who compiled it. It has seven speaking parts and seeks to give a direct appreciation and understanding of the Kingdom of Elves, as conceived in *The Silmarillion,* by Mankind of Middle-Earth, that is, ourselves.

The parts are designated by the position where they sit, being Officers of East, South and North, plus a Narrator, who represent humans; and Officers of South-West, West and North-West, who represent Glorfindel, Galadriel and Melian. Following a short statement from the East, who acts as leader, the company visualise themselves as travellers coming to the Grey Havens at dusk. As night comes they are greeted by the sight of a swan boat which appears out of a mist from the West. It is manned by a seemingly human woman and a High Elven Lord. Sailing with them, the company follows the course of the stars and as they travel their guides recount tales of the Early Days and describe the Valar. They feel the presence of these great beings building about them.

Finally, within sight of Valinor, they land on the island of Tol Eresséa, and there meet with representatives of the Elves who have passed into the West. They hear that although the Elves are unable to return to Middle-Earth in physical form, they wish to form deep relationships linking mind-to-mind with those individuals willing to travel thus in the imagination. Time is taken for individual dialogue and imaginary tokens are exchanged so that at a later time contact may again be made in this manner. To conclude, a simple dance is performed by the officers, which creates a "rainbow bridge" between themselves as representatives of Middle-Earth and the West. The rite is concluded by travelling back to the shores of Middle-Earth. The content can be augmented by judicious use of various readings and descriptions either from *The Silmarillion* itself and the related works of Tolkien, or the excellent glosses available such as *A Tolkien Bestiary* by David Day or *The Complete Guide to Middle-Earth* by Robert Foster. This in turn will suggest other types of journey or contact that may be undertaken.

THE VOYAGE WEST

EAST

Let the Artificer of Fire now cense the Temple.

[This is done.]

The night and the sea speak to us of Mystery – the mystery we behold as we contemplate the indigo night sky strewn with countless stars and remember the tales of lands beyond the Western seas. My Companions, join with us now in your hearts and imaginations to make this journey. We ride on a quest answering the strange summons which drew us forth.

[Music I: "Fantasia on a Theme" by Thomas Tallis (Vaughan Williams) suggested. The first three sections of music are from this piece.]

NORTH

We have travelled many miles these past days. Some of us have left behind the comfort and safety of our homes to make this journey.

SOUTH

And there are those of us whose home is the road. Yet each lord and lady, whether they count themselves adventurer, artist, bard or magician, has, at the request of he who called us together, brought with them one object – personal and special to serve as a token for a yet unrevealed purpose.

NORTH

We have walked individual paths yet have we joined to form this noble Company. During the nights we have drawn close to the camp fire to share with food and wine tales and songs of far-off times – to hear once more of the deeds of heroes – of their quests and the loves which inspired their hearts.

As we listened our imaginations soared and we dreamt of those times and of the parts we might have played in the shaping of Middle Earth.

SOUTH

The day is drawing to a close as we near our destination. We are wrapped in thick cloaks against the chill of this late spring day. Our horses are lightly lathered and their manes lift EAST gently in the breeze. The air is tangy with salt, the smell excites them and we dismount, leaving them to graze nearby as we make our way down into the Havens. We come to the inlet which marks the way to the sea in silence as our eyes and ears search for some sign that our journey shall be continued.

NARRATOR

The hills that surround the inlet are bare of all but the sparest vegetation and they fall away steeply as rugged cliffs into the deep natural harbour of Mithlond, the Grey Havens. As we look westward we can see the mighty rocks that mark the mouth of the Gulf of Lhún and beyond them lies the Western Sea. We see only the ruins of some buildings that once were part of the community of Elven shipwrights – yet there does remain intact an ancient wharf of strong, wide, wooden timbers.

The sun is lower in the West and the day begins to pass from us. Now the golden orb of Anar slips beneath the rim of the horizon on her journey into the Underworld from which she arises reborn each dawn. A light mist has come up from the sea and lies all about us.

EAST

It has been many years since the last of the Elves passed from these lonely shores into the West and I fear, my friends, that I have led you through these past days and nights merely on the strength of a dream.

SOUTH

What quest has not had at its heart a dream? You have held from us the nature of the quest. Will you speak now of it?

EAST

That vision shall never fade from my inner sight. I awoke from a troubled sleep with the vivid memory of the sea and a fair garden filled with trees bearing leaves of silver and gold and standing therein a wondrous woman – she was tall and clothed in white and silver; her hair the richest gold and her eyes … her eyes were filled with the light of the stars. She spoke and bade me to gather together a company of women and men whose courage and vision I knew and trusted to bring them on this eventide to these Havens.

As I woke the name "Lorien" came into my mind and I realised that in my dream I had looked upon the Lady Galadriel who journeyed from this place so long ago – leaving behind the fading woods of Lothlórien to seek peace after her many years spent here in Middle-Earth

Now as I gaze upon these empty shores I wonder if it were but a dream created by my heart's longing that such a people might yet exist beyond the known lands of the Earth. In this hour I am filled with doubt.

SOUTH

Yet we have followed you willingly, my lord. And it gladdens our hearts to stand in this place so renowned in legend though it is deserted now – no more do the Elven Shipwrights dwell on these shores – building and tending with love their boats to carry the Firstborn over the Western Sea to Valinor the Undying Land…

NARRATOR

As we stand gazing upon the misty waters we hear the sound of a fair horn and see approaching us up from the sea a wondrous boat – the like of which has not been seen near these shores for many years. Shaped in the image of a mighty swan with half-lifted white wings, eyes of jet set in amber and a beak of burnished gold. Her white sails bear the sigil of two trees upon a green hill – one silver, one golden. Silently now she slips through the water and comes up to the wharf.

We see within the stern of the swan-boat two noble figures clad in grey and white. There is something about them and the boat which seems almost insubstantial as if there were a mysterious barrier between us … Yet as we move forward to meet them this sense of strangeness passes. The couple disembark from the boat and we see them with the hoods of their grey cloaks thrown back. They stand before us – a dark-haired woman and a tall golden-bearded High Elven Lord. Their eyes shine as if lit by starlight and the wisdom held within belies their youthful appearance.

NORTH-WEST

I bring you greetings in the name of Manwé and Varda. I am Melian, of the Maiar, who was with Lord Thingol queen amongst the Gray-Elves of Beleriand during the Ages of Stars. My companion is the Lord Glorfindel of the Noldor, Councillor to the Lord Elrond who departed these shores at the end of the Third Age with those of Imladris and the Lady Galadriel.

SOUTH-WEST

In her name, travellers, I bid you now, if you are willing, to depart these shores and sail with us beyond the confines of Middle-Earth.

EAST

Lady and Lord – beyond all my expectations is this manifestation – I gladly will accompany you! What say you, my companions?

NORTH

The Company so wills to travel on and thus follow the Quest ...

SOUTH

Into the unknown mists of the West.

SOUTH-WEST

So be it.

NARRATOR

We board the swan-boat and it slips away from the shore as if guided by invisible hands; carrying us first down to the sea and then westward into the gray mists. The mist feels cool and clammy and so we wrap our cloaks about us. The boat moves with grace and speed over the calm sea. As we look about us the mists begin to clear and above our heads the vault of heaven is visible – deep indigo blue shimmering with the diamond radiance of the countless stars.

[Music II: During this music the Officers of the East, South and North come forward to the central altar and the Officers of the NW and SW turn towards the West as though standing in the prow of a boat. At end of the music officers of NW and SW turn to face the others.]

EAST

My lady, how do we sail and by what stars? I have long studied the lore of the sea and am confounded by the art that has built this ship and guides its course!

NORTH-WEST

Noble Lord, know that when the World was Changed following the Doom of Númenor, Men sought in vain for the Undying Lands – for no matter how far west they sailed they found only lands like to their old lands, subject to Death.

SOUTH-WEST

And those that sailed furthest set but a girdle about the Earth and returned weary at last to the place of their beginning – saying that indeed the World is round and the True West but a tale believed only by children and fools. So the peoples of Middle-Earth grew enslaved by their own narrowness of vision. Yet we have learned that there still remain those who would escape this enslavement – many who dare to think, to question and to dream – caring little that they may be counted fools!

NORTH-WEST

Yet the West was not denied, only hidden outside of the World by the art of the Valar. Through knowledge of star-lore a mariner might still find that Straight Road and the new world would fall away, the old world and the path of memory of the West return, as it were as a mighty bridge invisible that passed through the air of breath and of flight to come finally to the shores of Tol Eresséa and beyond to Valinor.

SOUTH-WEST

This night we follow that Straight Round beyond the world of Men.

EAST

Yet too is it not said that having passed into the West no human may return to Middle-Earth?

SOUTH-WEST

This is true and so it is to Tol Eressëa we travel and there by the grace of the Valar likewise a Company of the Eldar will come out of Valinor to meet with you. Therefore you will not truly enter the Undying Lands, only come close by its shores and thus be free to return ere morning to your home shores.

EAST

I feel confounded by you, noble Lady and Lord, for until this night I had thought of Elves as simple woodland spirits.

[NW and SW here may tell some of the history of the Elven folk through selected passages from the Silmarillion.]

[Music III]

SOUTH

You have told us of the Eldar but these Valar of whom you speak – are they Gods and Goddesses?

[Invocation of the Valar]

NORTH-WEST

In ignorance Men have thought them so – but no, though they are mighty beyond our understanding there burns within each of us whether Valar, Maiar, Elf or Man – a Divine Spark. As we continue our journey westward we shall tell of the lore of the Valar.

They were first Beings of Pure Spirit created from the Flame Imperishable and the Thought of Eru Ilúvatar, the One. He names them Ainur, the Holy Ones.

SOUTH-WEST

It came to pass that Ilúvatar called together the Ainur and spoke to them of a mighty theme and said, "Of the Theme I have declared to you, I will now that ye make in harmony together a Great Music."

NORTH-WEST

From out of this music came a Vision like a globed Light in the Void. Ilúvatar gave this Vision life and it became Arda – the World That Is. The Ainur looked upon this creation and were amazed. And many for love of this new place took leave of Ilúvatar and entered into it. The condition Ilúvatar made of them was that their power be henceforth contained and bounded in the World, and that they should remain in it until it is deemed complete, so that they are its Life and it is theirs.

They laboured long to shape the World as a habitation for the Children of Ilúvatar to come – the Eldar and Man. The greatest amongst these spirits numbered fifteen and thereafter were known as the Valar, the Powers of the World.

SOUTH-WEST

Of these – One who was in the Beginning the mightiest of the Ainur is no longer counted amongst the Valar, and his name is not spoken upon the Earth. His jealousy and pride led him to fall from splendour to contempt for all things save himself. He desired the Light and coveted Arda and all within it but realising he could not possess it for himself alone – turned to subtlety and attempted to corrupt and pervert to his will all he could. So came Evil into Arda. We of the Eldar have named him Morgoth, the Dark Enemy of the World.

NORTH-WEST

Glorfindel, dear brother, let us not dwell overlong upon this betrayal but speak instead of the Valar and as we sail invoke through our words the presence of these Mighty Ones about us.

[Here again more full descriptions can be read from either "The Silmarillion" or "A Tolkien Bestiary", in the following text designated by {.........}]

SOUTH-WEST

In the East is Manwé, the Wind Lord, First King of Arda: appointed as Vice-Regent of Ilúvatar and King of the Valar, Elves and Men. *{... ... ...}*

NORTH-WEST

Dwelling with Manwé in the domed Hall of Ilmarin, the Mansion of the High Air, is the Queen of the Valar – Vardar, Lady of the Stars. The Elves called her Elbereth, the Star Queen, and forever they sing to her by starlight. Her name is a talisman to all those who would have light dispel darkness.

[East and NW read poem commencing "Snow-white! Snow-white..." from The Lord of the Rings. East the first and last verses, NW the middle verses.]

SOUTH-WEST

Within the southern woods of Valinor dwells Oromé, the Huntsman and Tamer of Beasts. *{... ... ...}*

With him dwells Vána, sister of Yavanna. She is named the Ever-Young and dwells within a garden filled with birds and golden flowers.

NORTH-WEST

In the far West are the Halls of Mandos, the House of the Dead. Mandos is known as the Doomspeaker and is a Master of Spirits. He knows all the fates that were declared in the Music of the Ainur and watches the weaving of Destiny in the Great Tapestry fashioned by his spouse, Vairé, the Weaver. To his Mansion come the spirits of slain Elves to dwell within the Halls of Awaiting until the final days of Arda.

Dwelling alone west of West, upon the borders of the World is Mandos' sister Nienna, the Weeper. She does not weep for herself but mourns for every wound that Arda has suffered throughout the ages. *{... ... ...}*

SOUTH-WEST

In the North dwells Yavanna, Queen of the Earth, the Giver of Fruits. She loves all things that grow in the Earth. *{… … …}*

The spouse of Yavanna who shares with her the element of Earth is Aulé the Smith, the Maker of Mountains, Master of all crafts and deviser of metals and gemstones. *{… … …}*

NORTH-WEST

As we ride upon the Great Sea of Belegaer, we have pause to see below and all about us Ulmo, the Ocean Lord. *{… … …}*

SOUTH-WEST

These are the Valar that mark the Quarters and Elements but also I would tell of Nessa, the Dancer *{… … …}* and her spouse Tulkas, the Strong *{… … …}*

NORTH-WEST

Finally I shall speak of Lórien, the Dream Master, by his power comes forth all dreams and visions. He dwells in and is named for the fairest garden in all Arda. In memory of that place, beloved of all who have beheld it, the Lady Galadriel named her home within Middle-Earth – Lothlórien – though even in its full glory it was but a pale shadow of Lórien's garden.

His Lady is my Mistress, Esté the Gentle, healer of all hurts and weariness. She walks not by day but sleeps upon an island within the tree-shadowed lake of Lórellin. By night she walks with her Lord and together they weave the dreams of deep sleep. Grey is her raiment and rest her gift.

More would I say of Lórien and Esté but that must wait, for we near our destination. Look to the West!

[With a gentle gesture with her outstretched arm Melian turns with Glorfindel to face again the West while music plays for a time but is then faded to play softly underneath this section of narrative to the point where West stands before the Company.]

NARRATOR

Our swan-boat is approaching a beautiful island – it and the great land lying beyond seem to shimmer with an inner radiance so that we see them quite clearly despite the night. The beauty of the land takes our breath away as we come into shore alongside the wharf. Here upon the Lonely Isle we are so near and yet still far from the Undying Lands. We may not without leave travel further West yet the Light from that land and the re-kindled Trees of Laurelin and Telperion flows out across the waters.

We behold in the distance mighty mountains, their peaks white with snow set against the indigo star-lit skies and before them the eastern shores of Valinor are strewn with precious gems – diamonds, crystals and opals. There is the gate of a harbour cut from an arch of living sea-rock which marks Alqualondé, the Haven of the Swans, the city of the Teleri. We see their halls of pearl and crystal lit with many lamps and their swan-ships anchored within the harbour.

We disembark led by Melian and Glorfindel away from the shore, taking in the beauty all about us … we are surprised by the appearance of two nightingales who singing their sweet songs fly in greeting about Melian. Glorfindel explains that in the early days of Arda it was Melian who taught the nightingales their song and they are ever close to her.

We pass close by the tall White Tower of Avallóné and come shortly to a large wooden hall where fires are lit for our welcome. As we enter we behold within the hall a company of High Elves wondrously fair to our eyes; they are tall and noble with hair like spun gold, woven silver and polished jet. They are clad in silken robes with rich jewels upon their hands and within their hair. Their eyes, like those of our guides, seem filled with the light of the stars and indeed, their forms seem to shimmer in the soft lights of the room as if they walk in moonlight.

We are led forward by our guides who now take time to introduce us to those of the Company of the Eldar. We are initially reserved but after a few moments this breaks down and as the music plays we take that time to experience the Elves each in his or her own way.

[Music here is turned up by the Narrator; as it fades in completion the Officer of the West representing Galadriel steps forward.]

NARRATOR

From the recess of the Hall a figure comes forward. A tall and beautiful Elven woman clad simply in white and silver, her long golden hair is crowned by a circlet of white flowers and a small pale crystal is bound upon her brow. On her finger she wears a single ring, wrought of mithril and bearing a white stone flickering like a frosty star.

WEST

Travellers, I bid you welcome to this Hall. It has been my greatest hope to meet once more with representatives of the race of Men. I am Galadriel, Lady of the Noldor of the House of Finarfin.

EAST

Lady Galadriel, I am he to whom was granted the gift of your dream-message. If it be your will we would know why we have been summoned to this land from over the sea.

WEST

Yes, the time has come to speak of the purpose of this summons though the calling was not put forth by my will alone …

In these years following the close of the Third Age I have indeed found the rest and peace I longed for in the West and knew great joy in coming to know again my kindred after the long years of my exile.

Long had I dwelt in Middle-Earth and during my time within the Golden Wood of Lothlórien been deeply touched by those of your race. I did not forget. Through the power of Nenya, the Ring of Water, I was still granted the visionary gift and I watched with despair as the race of Men grew further away from wisdom – so many hearts turned cold and sight faded. How could I rest even in Valinor when I recalled that the Vision was meant for all the Children of Ilúvatar not the Eldar alone?

My heart was thus troubled and yet long I held only my own counsel until I found that I was not alone in my concern for the Secondborn. In time we joined together to form this Company yet knowing we were unable to return to Middle-Earth and lacking the art to make contact; we could only wait and pray that an answer would be found. Alone I came with this burden to the gardens of Lórien and walking there by moonlight I met with the Valar Esté and her Lord and opened myself to their wisdom and guidance.

We spoke and I learnt that the Valar had not forgotten Middle-Earth although they no longer walked those lands in physical form but watched the unfolding story of the World and Men and they too were troubled. For it seemed that the servants of the Enemy had returned in new and more subtle guises and now were in essence the rulers of Middle-Earth and thereby the Land and all living beings were threatened. Hearing this and knowing its truth I trembled for the fate of all and especially for the men and women of your race who should be the caretakers of the Earth, not assist in its destruction through apathy and worse.

Yet Lórien and Esté bade me not despair but to trust and wait – for the Valar were not idle in this matter. They counselled that those of the Eldar who so desired might aid in the healing work to come.

In my heart I believe that it was also the thoughts of such as yourselves that reached out over the Great Sea and called to us in your plight. These times may see a new alliance between Men and the Elves. I pray to Elbereth that this might be so!

EAST

Lady Galadriel, if I may speak for my companions – there may be within us a memory of those far-times when there was such an alliance, for in so many there lies deep within a yearning for the West and for the People of the Stars though our blood be human.

It may well be that each of our peoples have cried out for what has been lost and what might still be if the Vision of Ilúvatar is fulfilled. From that yearning has come this night - we love the Earth even as we dream of the West. Perhaps in time we may once more be joined as One World!

WEST

I am moved by your words, noble lord, and by the caring and love so written upon your faces. Remember too, that we stand not alone in this venture for it was the powers of Lórien that generated the visionary-dream wherein I sought to make contact with those women and men of Middle-Earth who would welcome this contact. And Esté sent forth her handmaiden, Melian, to navigate the Straight Road and so guide the swan-boat once more to the shores of Middle-Earth.

NORTH-WEST

Also, the power of Yavanna has called forth the energies of the living Earth to speak of its need for healing to the hearts of those who love, as she does, the land and all living things.

SOUTH-WEST

The Eagles and Hawks of Manwé have reached out carrying the thoughts of the Valar and the Eldar and sought to touch your minds and imaginations. It is not the way of the Valar to seek to compel or bind the Children of Ilúvatar – so this meeting and all that transpires in the future between our peoples must come from free will and the love we bear one another.

WEST

Our people too have brought out of Valinor our tokens to exchange with yours that as we depart this Isle – you to the East and we to the West – the alliance that has been begun this night may develop through these individual contacts and form new links between Middle-Earth and the West. What may come of these friendships may only be known to the Mind of Ilúvatar but greatly we desire that we may function as channels of healing and succour to our lost birthplace. It may well be that a new song arises from this night to celebrate the birth of the Fifth Age!

And so I bid you – each to seek within for this contact.

[Musical interlude for this process to take place. As the music fades Melian comes slightly forward bearing a large crystal, and holding it aloft she speaks, placing it upon the central altar.]

NORTH-WEST

Let us now join together in the dance to create a Rainbow Bridge of Light between us and thereby our lands – channelled through this Crystal of the Valar that healing may flow into Middle-Earth and the souls of Men be uplifted.

[Music begins and NW (Melian) and SW (Glorfindel) move to the central altar and take the hands of the Officers of North and South – with NW opposite South and SW opposite North as a polarity. They thus slowly circle the altar four times, visualising silver-white energy that is transmuted to Rainbow

Light. Following these circles they stop on the diagonals – SW and South to east of the altar and NW and North to west, so that there is a clear run through for Officers of East and West. They release hands and step back which is cue for a slight manual fade of the music.]

WEST

Of all of this Company, it was you who first opened your soul to the longing of the Eldar and, listening to my song, followed the vision of your dreams, and gathered this fair Company to make the long journey to these shores. Will you join me now in the dance?

EAST

With great joy I will, my Lady. *[Bowing.]*

[Music swell as she descends and the Officer of the East draws forward. Alone they move about the altar in a polarised dance wherein they focus the energy created previously into a glowing sphere above the altar and crystal – they do two circuits and on the third draw out so that on its completion the other Officers join in. The six make one circuit as if holding the Sphere of Light and further energise it holding one hand up, the other down.

The Officers then take the hands of those on either side of them, which results in a pattern of raised and lowered hands about the circle. They drop hands and the energy is sent forth to the Earth. Finally they loose hands – pause for a moment, and East and West return to their places.

The remaining dancers begin again to circle the altar with the South dropping out on the first circuit to stand in the south-east while the others continue for another circuit – then North drops out, remaining in the north-east and Officers of NW and SW continue for a half-circuit then halt and SW (Glorfindel) takes up the crystal, salutes Ilúvatar (above) and they complete their circuit and return (NW then SW) to their stations.]

[pause]

SOUTH-WEST

The night draws on and we must soon depart.

WEST

Indeed the time has come for each to return to their own lands. Thus I say to you all that we shall meet again in another time and place. May a star shine upon the hour of our next meeting. Remember always, elf-friends, that the Light of Ilúvatar is ever with you.

SOUTH-WEST

May the wisdom of Manwé enlighten your thoughts as you return once more to Middle-Earth and the mighty wings of his eagles protect you upon your paths.

NORTH-WEST

And may the love of Varda be within your hearts forever – as you walk beneath her Stars – remember her name.

[Music is begun (Clannad's "Marian" or similar) which continues softly through the closing narration and is turned up as it is completed.]

NARRATOR

Thus we are escorted by the Eldar down to the shore where awaits the swan-boat. We make our farewells … and board. Again Melian and Glorfindel are with us and we travel swiftly once again to the East through the craft of the Maiar – finding the Straight Road back to the known shores of Middle Earth.

[short pause]

All too soon we sight the land and come to shore once more at the Grey Havens. We disembark and take leave of our Guides, trusting that we shall see them again within the realms of the Far West and our dreams. The nightingales that have accompanied Melian sweetly sing as the sails of the swan-boat fill again and swell with the morning breeze. We watch upon the shore as they sail again to the West … as dawn breaks behind us the sails of the ship bearing the sigil of the Two Trees slips from our view.

***

9.
THE MAGICAL IMAGINATION

The more that participants use their imagination the more they are likely to get from a working such as this. Here are some examples of the kind of experience recorded by some who have taken part in similar pieces of work.

"When the symbols were carried round it seemed they drew from the ground behind them dark shadows of earth powers, which lay like a mist across the ground inside the circle."

"Our eyes were directed upwards into the blue sky, where a great bronze eagle flew, the sun striking light from his burnished wings. This fell in straight shafts down onto our heads, through and out the finger ends, onto the earth, to mingle with the shadows beneath our feet to form circular patterns of colour. The power was so strong as to be almost uncontainable."

"These circles of rainbow light became a bridge, across which came the goddess, Our Lady Star of the Sea, in her blue robe, with stars in her hair. Behind her crowded a host of dark bright apparitions, non-manifest materially, too ancient to take material form, expressions of ultimate wisdom and knowledge."

"When the Undying Shore was built, the magnetic force emanating from it was so strong that it was almost impossible not to let go and cross over the bridge and disappear into that golden land forever. It would have been so easy, and it took a definite act of will to create the cords of restraint."

"Then the whole scene dissolved into darkness, and I was left with a vast sense of loss and loneliness. It seemed this was indeed the secret garden, the golden land to which we all aspire to return, and which we once knew, Paradise lost."

"During the song saw a star figure with a wide cloak land at the North Pole and with the rhythm of the song and turning of the globe his cloak became a trail of wide rainbow ribbon which, as the planet turned, became a spiral encircling the Earth. Saw a light coloured spiral go up from the Earth like serpents of a caduceus. The outer spiral then shimmered from lines to a complete 'shell' - shimmering and live. The central spiral was like a seed inside. I thought this would become two trees."

"Apart from all this I realised how important one's own 'shire' is, I didn't even wish to cross the rainbow bridge – though I was happy to welcome any who crossed it to my side! I realised that in a way the 'immortals' have a different relationship with Earth than man. Man knows he must one day die and leave behind those things which he loves, what he calls beauty, what he calls home. Because of that every day is magnified, every beauty seen with greater clarity. Because man knows he must leave it, Earth becomes more dear, and more minutely observed."

"I feel the evening was a success in that a bridge was built to and from the West. The proof is all round me as I write, for there are golden, bright-eyed beings with me now. They are no figment of the imagination for they give off a warm energy."

"Since then I have had a vision of two great beings of light holding a brilliant sphere above them, each holding it with one arm, passing over a barren desert landscape, which becomes a green paradise of flowing streams and laughing, singing beings of all kinds."

"The Elves seem to say that simple, everyday events, such as taking food, should become linked to Ilúvatar by a realisation of Him as Creator. I get the feeling they think our time-oriented existence is pretty weird."

"Was very aware of what seemed to be a vast expanse of water between the Eastern and Western quarters and the image of the Rainbow Bridge was very strong and linked the two lands. When the horn was blown sensed the High Elves coming through the West and making a contact that was the most delicate of mental touches. Became aware of an energising of the brow centre and a sensation as though a star jewel or crystal was bound there upon a delicate mithral circlet. Aware of a gentle bell-like music too as they came through. There felt no sense of intrusion or muzziness of consciousness, but a clearing and uplifting."

"Unlike the elemental fairies with whom contact can be so fascinating and unbalancing because one drops back into an old undifferentiated form of consciousness, with these High Elves there comes a sense of wholeness and stepping forward into a cooperation with the unfolding evolution of consciousness. Their will and purpose links with that of Ilúvatar. They are intimately connected with star magic, the New Age, assisting from the True West in this transition period, aiding in the healing of Middle-Earth."

"I had one eye on the proceedings and the other on the figure building up behind me: Aragorn, in green cloak thrown back from his shoulders, and with jewelled crown and shining sword. It was then, I believe, that I began praying to Ilúvatar, 'Thy will be done, not mine,' over and over again. Peace came, but the power was really terrific."

"The vision of the rainbow road and the Undying Lands was very vivid. And I could see the white spires and rooftops of a city in the distance. Once the horn was blown, I felt rather than saw the beings coming in."

"The morning gave rise to a vision of the Rainbow Bridge, a sea in space leading into the new land of the West. It was like being an outrider on a wagon train 'going West' over this great rainbow sea. As to the One who is 'the Way', I remember thinking of part of the Opening of the Arch of Heaven - 'His the rainbow letters in the rich fermented milk.' One seemed to assist a vast convoy over the bridge from the Middle-Earth we know to Westernesse. One took loved ones, strangers, elementals, animals, all creation that was *willing* to live life the 'new way'."

From what has been here described it may thus become apparent that there is more to mythopoeic tales than idle fancy, and that in the right hands they have the power of individual and collective healing and regeneration, which is the province of White or High Magic. Something of the power of these images is indicated by an experience recounted by Professor Clyde Kilby in his small book *Tolkien and the Silmarillion.* This was a dramatisation of *The Lord of the Rings* presented by a group of schoolchildren, who had spent a whole year preparing the dialogue, scenery and costumes. He records that, despite it being only a fit-up performance in a school gymnasium, he was more than once moved to tears by it. And he was later told that the boy who played Frodo "did not emerge from his role for a month and then only reluctantly."

This only goes to show that magic is where you find it, and that it has its dangers for impressionable participants. It is indeed likely that the wholehearted imaginative involvement of the children produced a far more "magical" experience than a performance by a cast of professional actors would have achieved, where only the very gifted seem to have this ability. Clyde Kilby also felt that what he saw in Cheltenham that night surpassed anything that might be expressed in any film version. This raises the point that film (and especially television, where there is no group audience participation) is likely to destroy rather than stimulate the magical imagination.

We should, at this point, perhaps try to define just what "magic" and the "magical imagination" is. In the draft of a letter intended for Naomi Mitchison (#155 of his *Collected Letters* – ed. Humphrey Carpenter – Allen & Unwin 1981) Tolkien confessed that he felt he had been far too casual about "magic" and the use of the word, and that it was a very large and difficult question. He makes a distinction between the type of magic exercised by Sauron, and that which is used by Gandalf or the Elves. The former is used to dominate, subjugate, manipulate, the latter to provide help, such as make a fire with soaking wet faggots, or to lay on a pyrotechnic display. He thus considers it a neutral force that can be used for good or evil, although he hedges his bets and salves his Catholic conscience by saying that it is beyond the valid powers of men. He goes on to say that whilst Aragorn might have been reported to have used magic, it was really only a matter of healing mixed with pharmacy and hypnosis, that was in any case only reported by easily impressionable hobbits – apart from which Aragorn was anyway not a pure man, having Elven blood in his veins. One might suspect that in this matter the author "doth protest too much" and may have realised the weakness of his argument in not including this part in his final draft to Naomi Mitchison, who was an historical novelist (of *The Corn King and the Spring Queen* etc.,) who knew very well what magic was all about. She was one of the few serious critics to have reviewed *The Lord of the Rings* favourably (in the *New Statesman*) and Tolkien was touched enough to thank her personally and at length.

The thing is that Tolkien had a grasp of a far wider conception of the magical powers of the human mind than is apparent in the vulgar use of the word magic, which restricts it to the production of wonders along the lines of a stage illusionist, or travellers' tales of oriental fakirs. He reveals as much in his letter to Naomi Mitchison in his remarks upon Númenor and the Atlantis legends, in respect of how the "voyage west" represents a fundamental change in perceptive consciousness in terms of human accessibility to other modes of being.

That is to say, that there was what Tolkien calls a Downfall, before which the heavenly worlds and the earthly paradise of Valinor and Eresséa were upon the same plane as the world of men, but after the fall of Atlantis/Númenor both were removed from the physically attainable Earth, although the way west may still be open under certain circumstances. This metaphysical state of affairs he felicitously describes as the way directly west as might be observed from a flat and mythopoeic earth. The return to the original starting point is enforced only when going west on a spherical physical world. This could be construed as the difference between magical and mystical consciousness, and on the other hand on ordinary human consciousness that is consticted to physical perception.

Mystical consciousness is the mode of perception of the angelic world of Valinor. Magical consciousness is the mode of perception of the paradisal world of Faery. The modus operandi of both lies within the imagination, which, it should be added, is also the means of interpretation of physical perception, as Coleridge described in his concept of the Primary Imagination. The Secondary Imagination, which in his view was the mode of high artistic expression, is also the mode of the magical and mystical perceptions of the human mind if these are sympathetically developed and not confused with wish fulfilment dreams or arbitrary fancy.

It is this which ensures the perennial appeal of mythopoeic stories, from the Odyssey to Terry Pratchett and thence to Harry Potter. Deep calls unto deep, whatever the apparent shallowness of surface.

10.
THE WORLD OF FAERY

Apart from the great mass of manuscript that comprised *The Silmarillion* and various off-shoots from it through the scholarship of his son Christopher and others, there are very useful pointers to the Elven tradition (or in more general terms, the World of Faery), in Tolkien's celebrated essay *On Fairy Stories.* More directly revealing perhaps than his essay, for it speaks with the language of the imagination rather than the intellect, is his own fairy story *Smith of Wooton Major.*

On Fairy Stories

He begins his essay by defining what the real folk of faery are NOT! He quotes the Oxford English Dictionary to show its utter inadequacy in this respect, and he shows scant respect for literary traditions, whether of Drayton or Shakespeare, that depict cute fairies of diminutive size. He considers Drayton to be responsible for the worst fairy story every written, with Oberon's palace described as having walls made of spiders' legs, windows made from cats' eyes, and a roof of bats' wings. He also quotes Andrew Lang's scorn for late nineteenth century authors and their sermonising "fairies of polyanthuses and gardenias and apple-blossom."

For a more accurate picture of faery we have to go back to the older tradition of writers such as Thomas the Rhymer, who describes the Queen of Elfland riding on a milk white steed, swifter than the wind, and of enchanting beauty. This beauty is part of faery magic, for they are able to present themselves other than they are. The pride and beauty they put on – which may be but a reflection of the human observer's desires – can serve, for good or for ill, to play upon human carnal and emotional susceptibilities.

Stories about elves or faeries themselves are comparatively rare, for the essence of most stories lies in the adventures of a human who wanders into their Perilous Realm. It is a world of a richness and strangeness that defies accurate reporting and where asking too many questions may cause the gates of vision to be shut forever.

He spends some time analysing the blind alleys entered into by scholars seeking "origins" of faery-tale themes. Their true origin is like a great cauldron of inspiration from which a soup can be ladled into various bowls of story, some of them legendary and some quasi-historical.

Nor does he have much sympathy for the assumption that the stories are particularly suited to children, or that children are particularly suited to them. This commonly held association is, in his view, a cultural historical accident. A faery story worthy of the name is worth being read by adults, who are likely to get far more from it than children can.

This leads naturally to the final and most important part of his essay. What is it that a faery story can offer to listener or reader? Why, if written with due art and skill, should the faery story not be able to stand on at least level terms with any other form of literature – rather than be relegated to juvenile fiction?

Writing fantasy is arguably a higher form of art when it combines the imaginative faculty with images of things that are "not to be found in our primary world at all, or are *generally believed* not to be found there." The italics are mine, indicating Tolkien's belief in this mode of reality. A belief that is not shared by those who think that the material world, presented to our physical senses, is the only reality there is.

Fantasy has an arresting strangeness, and this fact is an element that repels or frightens people who dislike any expansion of their own limited conception of the world. It is they, in Tolkien's view, who stupidly and even maliciously try to brand fantasy as idle dreaming, mental disorder, delusion or hallucination.

Writing fantasy is also a very difficult art. It is not sufficient for the writer to juggle nouns and adjectives in a hat and produce the merely fantastical – bizarre images which carry no emotional charge. This level may well be the standard of work of a great deal of run-of-the-mill fiction, but it produces no internal resonance of an unseen reality. Similarly with painting. A kind of fantastic imagery is easy to produce, but the result often either silly or morbid.

Earlier in his essay Tolkien, in seeking a definition or synonym for Faery, had hit upon the word Magic. He has in mind a wider context than what he calls "vulgar devices of the laborious, scientific, magician." He sees it rather as a type of exalted mood or imaginative empowerment.

This would certainly be close to what another great mystic of the world of faery, George Russell ("A.E.") has described in his little classic *The Candle of Vision.* It is to be found also in some of the works of W.B.Yeats and Fiona McCleod, although magic or faery does not necessarily have an exclusively Irish or Celtic ambience.

He returns to this conception of magic in the latter part of his essay, where he evokes a similar mode of imaginative experience, the drama. Not that he has a great deal of time for theatrical performance, which often works *in spite of* rather than *because of* its nature. This he calls a kind of bogus, or substitute, magic. There is more to magic and perception of the world of faery than in what Coleridge calls "a willing suspension of disbelief" when the curtain goes up.

Tolkien coins the term Faerian Drama. This is an ability to produce fantasies within the minds of men "with a realism and immediacy beyond the compass of any human mechanism." It has the effect of transporting the individual into the faery world. And although it has sometimes been compared to dreaming, or even identified with it, it is a dream that some *other* mind is weaving.

In Tolkien's view, in a very significant passage, the human being is being deluded. Although whether this is the elvish intention is open to question. Certainly they are not deluded themselves within this transaction. For them, it is a form of art. A magical art if you will. For the world so depicted is not one within which they themselves live. The primary world of reality, for Tolkien, is the same for elves and for men. It just happens to be differently valued and perceived by the two races of created being.

Preferring to avoid the word "magic" because of its misleading and historically dubious associations, and not much enamoured of the psycho-philosophical term "secondary belief", Tolkien prefers to use the word "enchantment." Magic, in its vulgar sense, claims to produce changes in the primary world about us. Enchantment, on the other hand, evokes a secondary world in which faery and human can meet.

Writing or telling faery stories, in Tolkien's view, is the nearest human equivalent to this elven enchantment.

Whether approached from the human or the elven side, enchantment is not, like the low forms of magic, a self-centred desire for power. Nor is it a vehicle for glamour, bewitchment or delusion. Rather is it a seeking for shared enrichment, with partners in cooperative and delightful enterprise.

Whilst some may choose to think fantasy a juvenile folly, Tolkien sees it as a natural human activity which neither destroys nor insults reason. Here he cites a few lines of *Mythopoeia* a long poem that he once wrote to his friend C.S.Lewis in rebuttal of Lewis' remark that myths were lies and therefore worthless, even though "breathed through silver." It is a witty restatement of much that Coleridge formulated in seeing man as a sub-creator whose imaginative powers are a God-given reflection of the original Divine Creative Fiat.

Whilst of course fantasy can be abused or carried to excess, like any other human quality, it is certainly not a symptom of the softening of the brain or deliquescence of the critical faculties. On the other hand the inappropriate use of the critical faculties for an analytical study of fairy stories, is the one way to deprive oneself of all their potential rewards.

These rewards Tolkien summarises under the headings of Recovery, Escape and Consolation.

Recovery is gaining a clear view of the world in which we live. The word can also be used in the sense of a renewal of health. It is a means of, in the words of William Blake, "cleansing the doors of perception." That which may have become blurred by over-familiarity can be restored to pristine wonder by a short holiday within the realms of fantasy. However, faery stories have an additional quality in this respect. In dealing with simple and fundamental things, such as clay, stone, wood, iron, trees, grass, horses (winged or otherwise), these too are seen in a new light, bringing back perhaps the direct perceptions of colour, shape, and brightness that were wondrous to us in childhood but which have since become staled by custom and concept.

Escape is the breaking free from the prison house of modern civilisation. Whilst there is a school of thought that chooses to condemn what it calls "escapism from the real world" it rather begs the question as to what the "real world" and its accepted values really are. Tolkien had scant regard for a young colleague at Oxford who welcomed the proximity of the British Motor Corporation factory as bringing a slice of "real life" to the city of dreaming spires. Nor did he see any necessarily pejorative sense in the word "escape." If one were in a prison or under an oppressive regime then escape would seem to be the natural and sensible thing to do. Is being a collaborator with the dark forces of Mordor any more admirable? However, the deeper side of the faery story concerns escape not merely from the noise, stench and extravagance of modern industrial society. It is concerned with the deeper issues of human existence – hunger, thirst, poverty, pain, sorrow, injustice, death. The means by which we may escape from them is by the imaginative journeying to other realms of being. Of conceiving of talking animals or understanding their proper speech. Also an appreciation of mortality and time - as compared to endless serial living - or of the unchanging and immortal.

Consolation is the convention of the happy ending, which Tolkien prefers to call a "good catastrophe" - for it tends to be a sudden miraculous turn of events that has almost a metaphysical underpinning. It is a final universal Joy beyond the parameters of the known world. Beyond all the wild events of the preceding story. And is even capable of casting a glow of glory backwards into the earlier parts of the tale.

This last consideration brings Tolkien back to the cast of mind of every teller of tales who seeks to evoke a secondary world. Deep in their hearts they hope that they are drawing upon a quality that is derived from an underlying reality that their imaginative world may serve to reveal, be it only by a sudden glimpse.

In this the faery story may come close to a religious revelation, and Tolkien, as a committed Christian, approaches this possibility with some humility and reserve. He goes so far as to compare the gospels to a faery story, with their many marvels, all implying a mythopoeic significance, with, at the end, the inconceivably "good catastrophe" or happy ending of the glorious resurrection.

The gospels are thus the epitome of the fantasy writer's art, a beautiful story that turns out in all senses to be true, an historical narrative that loses nothing of its mythical or allegorical significance. If such is the case: "Art has been verified. God is the Lord, of angels, and of men – and of elves. Legend and History have met and fused." In this respect, the humble writer of stories may perhaps dare to conceive that by the use of his God given talents, his stories may have contributed something toward the enrichment of the Creation as a whole.

Smith of Wooton Major

We may now turn to an exemplification of Tolkien's views in his story *Smith of Wooton Major*. It is the story of a blacksmith who, as a boy, receives a faery gift in the form of a silver star. He has unknowingly eaten it at a children's party, and it appears (for those who can see it) upon his brow. It allows him to visit Faery-land and much of the story concerns his adventures there.

Not that these adventures are in the form of a great heroic quest. He simply journeys within those lands and encounters some of the beings there. That is to say, he is a learner and explorer, not a warrior in these realms. Exploration is not without its dangers, although with the star upon his brow, he is guarded from greater evils and lesser evils avoid him of their own accord. His name in Faery is Starbrow, although in the human world it is Smith, after his family calling as a blacksmith.

Faery-land appears to be an island, with high mountains at its centre. It would thus seem to have something in common with the Elf haven of Eresséa in *The Silmarillion.* All that is said of this is that he once saw a white ship of elven mariners, tall and terrible, who had been sailing upon the Sea of Windless Storm, engaged in battles on the Dead Marches of which men know nothing.

On another occasion, after having lost his way in a grey mist, he comes upon a great tree growing out of a shadowy hill which forms its root. It ascends high into the sky, shining golden like the noon sun, and is covered simultaneously with countless leaves and flowers and fruits, all different. He only came upon this vision once however, in spite of trying several times to find it again.

Another time he comes upon a deep valley in which is a smooth lake that glows red like a sunset. Within it fiery creatures swim amongst weeds that have the appearance of flames, but the surface is as hard and slippery as ice. When he tries to walk across it a great wind arises and sweeps him to the shore and up into the surrounding hills like a dead leaf, until he manages to cling on to a young white birch tree. After the wind has passed every leaf has been stripped from the tree and it stands weeping tears like rain. He tries to commiserate with the tree and to thank it, but feels an answer from it travel up his arm, simply telling him he does not belong there and should go away, never to return, for the wind is hunting him.

One day after much searching he manages to find a pass through the mountains to the centre of the island. Here there is a beautiful valley, the Vale of Evermorn. The air is clearer than any air on Earth and bubbling brooks and waterfalls cascade down the hillsides towards a river, full of lilies, next to which, upon a greensward, maidens are dancing to the singing of elven voices.

The dancing stops and a young maiden approaches him. She asks if he has no fear of what the Faery Queen might say if she knew that he had come upon their revels. Nonetheless she invites him to be her partner and leads him into the ring for a dance of which his impression is of incredible swiftness, power and joy. At the end she stops and picks a white flower and puts it in his hair. Bidding him farewell she says that perhaps they might meet again, with the Queen's permission.

Some years later, by earthly time, he is invited into the Queen's presence, by a long and winding way that is frequently obscured by mist and shadow. It leads to a high place under the stars where he sees the Queen standing before him in all her glory. She had no need of crown or throne but stands with a white flame burning above her head, surrounded by a great host shimmering like stars. Suddenly the host disappears leaving the two of them alone.

Looking into her face he recognises the maiden he had once danced with on the green. They stand talking together for some time, mostly without need of words, and he learns many things, of grief and of joy. Finally she gives him a message that he must to convey to the Faery King. It say that "he time has come" and with it comes "a choice."

He kneels and she lays her hand on his head, and he feels a great peace come upon him. Then the dawn breaks and the Queen is gone, but for the echo of an elven trumpet call high in the hills.

This marks the end of Smith's ability to visit Faery land, for the time has come to give back the star upon his brow. Upon his way home he meets the Faery King who has for some years walked among men in the guise of a human, known to the residents of Wooton Major as Alf (a name which is closely akin to Elf), the apprentice to a former Master Baker.

Smith, with heavy heart, agrees to render up the star to Alf, so it can be placed within the next cake, at a festival that occurs only every twenty-four years. As he has freely given up the star he is allowed the choice of who the next eater and bearer of the star will be, and he chooses his nephew, Tim of Wooton Minor. As he gives up the star so he is conscious of Venus, the evening star, shining brightly and riding closely by the Moon.

Throughout all of this story there is much traditional faery lore. It lies back of the actual descriptions of the secondary world of the story, in the dynamics of power that are hinted at, with the impression that Faery land can be an awesome place and a dangerous one for those who do not respect its laws.

The Adventures of Tom Bombadil

Tom Bombadil appears in *The Lord of the Rings* as a powerful kind of figure, at one with nature, and somehow separated from and even unconcerned with all the dramas that are going on around him. He proves however to be friendly and helpful to the hobbits. He also appears in an episodic narrative poem of some 130 lines called *The Adventures of Tom Bombadil* whose composition pre-dates *The Lord of the Rings* by some years. It later provides the title for, and is the leading poem in a slim volume of verses, in which those entitled *The Hoard, The Sea-Bell,* and *The Last Ship* are of particular interest from the point of view of faery.

Bombadil himself appears to have been one of a number of miscellaneous good spirits who came to inhabit Middle-Earth. Tom himself is remarkable for his dress of blue coat, green girdle, leather breeches, tall hat with a swan's feather, and yellow boots. He is always singing or rhyming, walking about the meadows near the River Withywindle, gathering buttercups or tickling bees. He is an inhabitant of the Old Forest and even master of it. He is married to the golden haired Goldberry, the River-woman's daughter, who is as beautiful as an elven queen, dressed in silver and green with shoes like fish scales and whose singing is like the birds. The rhymed adventures tell of his marriage to Goldberry; and of him sporting merrily with those who might prove something of a danger to others, such as the old Willow-man, the Badger-folk, and even an old Barrow-wight. In another series of verses he goes boating, talking to the wild creatures he meets on the way down the river, the wren, the robin, the kingfisher, the otter, the swan – and then sails over a wier to spend three days in the realms of men, most of them spent carousing with Farmer Maggot.

The Hoard is an evocation of buried treasure of strange provenance, fashioned by dwarves for the crowns of elves, guarded by an ancient dragon and a dead king, that has immediate relevance to *The Hobbit* and the adventures of Bilbo Baggins. It also has resonances with similar stories in folk lore and legend. One such that comes to mind is the treasure of Elinas, King of Albany (or Scotland), who married a faery. For betraying a promise he made to her he was confined in a mountain on Bamborough Head with all his treasure. This treasure is later guarded by a dragon and watched over by Palastine, one of his half-faery daughters, until such time as it may be released for the freeing of Jerusalem.

The Sea-Bell is an evocative story of finding a white shell upon the beach of a bell like shape. On shaking the shell a soft chime is heard within which is answered by the appearance of a boat gliding silently by, grey and empty, into which the finder of the shell leaps. He is borne away in a mist to the shores of a strange land, past a sea-bell clanging in the swell beside a dangerous reef.

The sand of the shore is like pearl dust with shells of opal, coral, emerald and amethyst under great pale cliffs, white under the moon, in which there are dark weed-curtained caves. The ambience is not dissimilar, in its sense of wondrous beauty yet concealed dangers, to the wanderings into faery of Smith of Wooton Major. The adventurer passes inland to a fair country of permanent twilight and comes to a slow-running river and a blue, glassy pool. Here wild creatures are to be seen: white hares, voles, moths "with lantern eyes," and badgers staring out of their holes. Over all is the light sound of dancing and music in the air, which is ever elusive as to its source.

He makes himself a green mantle of rushes and river-leaves, fashions a tall wand and a golden flag, and puts a crown of flowers on his head. Then standing upon a mound he calls out for the hidden dancers to reveal themselves, for he stands like a king among them. He is immediately struck down, blinded.

He can now only crawl towards a wood, where he lies in dead leaves surrounded by owls, beetles, spiders and fungal puffballs for a year and a day, bereft of half his wits. Eventually, a pale light dawns upon him, and lank and grey haired, with darkness like a hovering bat overshadowing him, and a withering wind chilling him, with only briars to cover himself, he makes his painful way back to the shore, to the sound of mewing seabirds and the barking of seals.

The boat awaits him, by which he returns to the world of men, but only to find houses shuttered against him and roads empty. In drizzling rain he casts away the shell, a few grains of sand remaining in his hand, and takes up the life of a ragged wanderer, talking to himself, and shunned by all he meets. In some respects he is a lesser form of the Ancient Mariner, but even worse cursed than he, for he has attempted to take the world of Faery by storm, and to have acted presumptuously towards it. All this is a far cry from the sentimental tinsel-winged image of fairyland.

The Last Ship bears a closer relationship to the events in *The Silmarillion* and the departure of the Elves from Middle-Earth. An earth maiden by the name of Fíriel witnesses the last white ship pulling out of the estuary, with its golden beak and oars, piloted by swans. Three elven kings or queens are among the elven folk on board, who sing a farewell lament to the sound of harps in time to the swing of the oars.

She calls to ask where they are going, to be told it is back to Elvenhome where the White Tree grows and the Star shines upon the foam. They say they have one place left upon the ship if she wishes to join them, but as she takes a step foward she feels her feet sink into the clay of the river bank and realises that she cannot do so, for she is a daughter of Earth.

She returns to her hearth and home, a mortal life of work in a smock of russet brown, rather than an immortal life in the jewelled robes of elf land. And now no more westward bound ships are to be seen, or elven voices heard over mortal waters. It is a sad elegy but one that recognises the immutable difference between the First and Secondborn of Ilúvatar, a gap which very few can cross.

11.
WHEN WE DEAD ARISE

Leaf by Niggle

Although Tolkien professed little time for allegory or for the revelation of authors within their works, by his own admission this little story has allegorical and autobiographical elements within it. It came to him virtually complete one morning upon waking, and he wrote it down at a sitting, later describing it as the most effortless piece of writing that he had ever undertaken. This was about 1939/40 and some five years later when asked to contribute something of a Catholic interest to the *Dublin Review,* he sent it along, and it was published in their January 1945 issue.

It contains an allegorical description of his experience in trying to reconcile his vocation as a writer of mythopoeic fantasy with that of his professional duties as a university don and other calls upon his time. However, it goes beyond such frustrations of physical life to an after-death condition where, in a purgatorial condition, he comes to terms with how he failed to learn certain necessary lessons in physical life. Then, having assimiliated these lessons, he is able to pass on toward a heavenly vista. Its scenario is thus in accord with a Roman Catholic post mortem world view and thus was eminently appropriate for the requirements of the *Dublin Review.* It is also an excellent and interesting little story in its own right, with a certain resonance to C.S.Lewis' similar light hearted but fundamentally serious speculation *The Great Divorce.*

Niggle is a painter, but not a very successful one, because he always has so many other things he has to do, many of which he regards as just a time consuming nuisance. One may therefore see here Tolkien, the writer, impatient with a number of his professional administrative duties, and the need to take in school examination papers for marking as a means to make ends meet. However, the same elements occur in the lives of most of us, confronted with contending demands of duty and desire, so the story has wider application than just a subjective condition peculiar to Tolkien.

Niggle wants to paint a great picture of a tree but finds himself frustrated because he is only able to paint leaves. This is mainly because he becomes so involved with depicting an individual leaf that he can never get round to completing the whole tree. This does reflect a problem that Tolkien had with his vast vision in becoming too closely involved with small parts of it.

C.S.Lewis has told of Tolkien's obsessive perfectionism, that made it extremely difficult to get a finished manuscript out of him, whether academic or fictional. In the face of the slightest criticism, whether from another or self generated, he might well virtually scrap a whole work and start from the beginning again. Thus the choice of the name Niggle as a form or alter-ego would not have been at all inappropriate for him.

The choice of a tree to represent his vision was sparked by his great love of trees in general, and more particularly his concern for a beautiful old tree outside his home that was in danger of being felled. Nonetheless the tree is also a most appropriate symbol of his artistic vision, which at that time was still largely unpublished and seemed likely to remain so.

Niggle's problems increase as he gets more and more involved with his tree painting, that gets larger and larger and more and more complicated. He also has various demands put upon him, at first by neighbours seeking help, and then by the interference of an officious Inspector who says his canvas, wood and waterproof paint would be more usefully employed patching up peoples' houses damaged by flood. This thought must haunt the thoughts of many a creative artist before success or recognition are attained.

Things get worse when a mysterious Driver calls, of similar unsympathetic aspect to the Inspector, who requires him to go upon a journey to an undisclosed destination. Although not explicitly stated, it is the last journey that all of us take, in a hearse to our own funeral. It is not the end of conscious life however, for Niggle finds himself taken to some kind of institution, where he is considered to be sick in some way. He now has to spend his time in a Workhouse Infirmary, where he is given bitter medicine by unpleasant officials, and is put to working hard for stated hours at boring jobs, either in the dark or in rooms with no outward looking windows.

However, although the situation never gets any more pleasant he does in the end begin to feel a certain sense of satisfaction at doing all he is set to do as best as he can. He is finally released from these chores and the doctors in charge ordain complete rest for him, in the dark. The Purgatorial experience has come to an end and he now awaits a judgement upon the state of his soul.

As he lies in the dark he overhears two mysterious Voices reviewing his case, who might be regarded either as aspects of his own conscience or more objectively as angelic overseers. In the end the Voices agree that he is perhaps now ready to be admitted to more gentle treatment, with a view to being admitted to the King's Feast.

Once more he goes upon a journey, only this time he is guided by a friendly Porter rather than forced against his will by a stern

Driver. After a journey on a little train he alights, to find his favourite bicycle waiting for him, upon which he rides off over a green and pleasant countryside. This would appear to be the outer reaches of Heaven.

The inner reaches of Heaven are heralded by his coming upon the actual Tree that he had laboured so long to paint. It is his vision of perfection and beauty that is alive and growing as a real tree, with birds singing and nesting within it. Some of the birds also fly off towards a great Forest of similar trees, and there presumably the soul of Niggle will find everlasting bliss.

There we leave him, and take a look at conditions back on Earth. Here his efforts at painting are meeting with neglect – which might very well have seemed to be the likely fate of Tolkien's writing before his astonishing success in later years. As it was, *The Silmarillion* and other parts of "the great tree" were published posthumously. A town councillor and a schoolmaster discuss Niggle and his work. The officious bureaucrat thinks Niggle's life to have been absolutely valueless to society and that it would have been better if he had been set to communal labour or evenexterminated. The pedagogue thinks however that this is going rather too far, that there might conceivably be a use for the arts, even if not for the type of old fashioned private day-dreaming that characterised Niggle's work.

The only person who seems to show any sympathy for Niggle is an old acquaintance who had no idea that he painted. However one small fragment of his work is eventually hung in the town museum (*The Hobbit?)* but in the course of time the museum is burnt down, and with it the last evidence of Niggle's work on earth.

However, on the outskirts of the heaven worlds, two Voices may be heard giving some praise to Niggle's work as being one of the best introductions, for wandering souls, to the heavenly mountains.

12.
THE PRICE OF GLORY

The Homecoming of Boerhtnoth

Tolkien was, amongst other things, a scholar of Anglo-Saxon, and his professional academic works include research into such Anglo-Saxon and Middle English classics as *Beowulf* and *Gawain and the Green Knight*. Both these works have magical and faery elements but Tolkien's work with them remains in the sphere of the academic. He was however inspired to some creative activity by a the fragment of an Anglo-Saxon poem *The Battle of Maldon*.

In all three of these works Tolkien identifies elements that throw light upon the heroic spirit of the age of the northern warrior. The nub of this problem is the responsibility resting in the chief of warriors for the fate of those who have sworn allegiance to him. In Beowulf this is summed up in the exclamation of Wiglaf:

"By one man's will many must woe endure."

As a veteran of the 1st World War these thoughts may well have been engendered in Tolkien's experience of trench warfare and the role of those in politics and high command who sent thousands to their deaths in four years of deadlock in a hell of gas and shell, vermin, mud and disease.

In the case of Beowulf we have a hero boasting he will go alone, even unarmed, against monsters in order to enhance his own glory. In the event he succeeds in vanquishing the monster although at the cost of losing his own life. What he did not seem to consider was that by this rash if heroic attitude he was putting at risk the fate of those whom he was supposed to be rescuing from the monster.

With Gawain, we have a knight going out apparently certain death by having his head cut off by an ogre, in order to uphold the honour and dignity of Arthur's court. The fact that the Green Knight exemplifies some great nature force and that the story is a conflation to vaunt the laws of chivalry marks the difference in knightly perceptions between its fourteenth century date and the eighth century date of *Beowulf*. Gawain's fate is never really at risk except from elements of his own perfidy.

The story of Beorhtnoth is rather different as it is an account of an historical incident that occurred in 991 A.D.

Beorhtnoth was leader of the Anglo-Saxon territorial army who faced a large band of marauding Vikings ravaging the East coast of England. The Vikings were confined to an island in the river estuary and could only reach the mainland by a narrow causeway. Beorhtnoth decided to allow them to cross this causeway in order to assemble and fight a pitched battle. In the ensuing battle the Vikings won, and Beorhtnoth lost his life along with most of his companions. The consequences of this "honourable" decision to stage a "fair fight" had devastating and long lasting consequences. The Vikings extorted such sums of tribute money from King Ethelred the Unready that to this day more archaeological finds of English silver coins of that period are to be found in Scandinavia than in England itself.

The poetic fragment, *The Battle of Maldon,* describes Beorhtnoth's last stand, and a moving account it is. It contains within it two lines of implied criticism of the Saxon leader, which Tolkien translates as: "then the earl in his overmastering pride actually yielded ground to the enemy, as he should not have done."

The Anglo-Saxon word *ofermode* occurs in three other contexts in Old English with the meaning "pernicious pride" (once in a reference to Satan) although attempts have been made to interpret the word more in Beorhtnoth's favour, to mean something more like "great courage" or "magnanimity." However, the meanings "pride, arrogance, over-confidence" are given in the glossary to an edition of the poem edited by the scholar D.G.Scraggs.

It is just this point upon which Tolkien expands in his fragment of dramatic verse entitled *The Homecoming of Beorhtnoth,* in which two Anglo-Saxons are searching for the body of their dead lord amongst the slain to take him to Christian burial. One of them recalls the old pagan heroic sagas which present a vivid contrast to the stark reality that lies before them, of rotting bodies picked over by a few starving scavengers after the Vikings have left. However, they find their slain lord, load his body into a tumbril, and the piece ends with the sound of the monks of Ely chanting a requiem mass.

So much for Tolkien's short piece, which perhaps represents no great contribution to the vast extent of his creative works, but which has a resonance with a strange experience of my own. Long before I ever came upon this work of his I happened to attend a celebration of the 1000th anniversary of the Battle of Maldon, in 1991, upon the actual site.

It was the usual kind of historical re-enactment, ending with a fair number of local youths, appropriately dressed, belabouring each other with thinly disguised dustbin lids and broomsticks, and then falling down in mock-death.

At the end of such a display the accustomed way, or so I assume, of ending the piece is for the announcer on the public address system to make a mild joke, by proclaiming "Let the dead arise!", whereupon all the participants still lying in the field get up and go off for some deserved liquid refreshment. Certainly that was the formula used upon this occasion, although it was rendered by a girl who happened to have a resonant and evocative voice. Three times she called out this summons and I felt the hair on the back of my head stand up on end, for to my inner perception many dead were indeed arising from the ground where they had fallen a thousand years before.

No doubt this can be put down to idle fantasy fortuitously induced into a superstitious and impressionable mind – and there is no copper bottomed defence against such a charge. However, to my mind it was an instance of the magical imagination at work.

I spent a disturbed night, unable to keep Anglo-Saxons, so it seemed, from crawling in and out of my head. Not only that, I was profoundly affected by the thought of their leader Beorhtnoth and at the same time afflicted by a deep sense of guilt and remorse on his part, for which I could not account, but which it seemed I should try to assuage. It seemed out of proportion with simply having lost a battle.

To a large degree this was ameliorated on the following Sunday when a service was held at the local church to dedicate a commemorative window to the battle, and as it happened, a specialist choir had been invited from far afield to sing an ancient mass, dating from the Anglo-Saxon period.

It seemed to have an anodyne effect, although for some time I felt a bond of kinship with Beorhtnoth, and even learned parts of the poem off by heart, in the original Anglo-Saxon. This, as I say, might well be put down to my own private folly, but it was not until much, much later that I came upon Tolkien's emphasis upon that aspect of *The Battle of Maldon* that gives good reason for what had seemed to me excessive remorse on Beorhtnoth's part. May he now rest in peace.

Farmer Giles of Ham

It may be a fitting postscript to our survey of Tolkien's work to take account of the story of *Farmer Giles of Ham*, which, despite its light-hearted approach, makes a serious point that is not unconnected with the problems confronted by Beorhtnoth.

It is an early work, which at one time he thought might provide a companion story and follow up to *The Hobbit* in 1938. After an unpublished existence in various drawers, occasionally being taken out for readings to friends and children, it was eventually published in 1949, illustrated by Pauline Baynes, with whose work Tolkien was well pleased, gallantly going so far as to say that his text might well be considered as secondary to the tale told by the drawings.

Naomi Mitchison wrote to express her appreciation when it was published and Tolkien made due apologies to her for some of the anachronisms (such as a blunderbuss and Greek fire). He was wont to describe it as a "donnish little squib," as might well be assumed from its full title of *The Rise and Wonderful Adventures of Farmer Giles, Lord of Tame, Count of Worminghall and King of the Little Kingdom* which he also renders into dog Latin for good measure.

The action takes place in that historical period in England between the departure of the Romans and the coming of the Saxons. It is thus quite close to the time at which historians place the existence of King Arthur, conceived as a *dux bellorum* or "count of the Saxon shore."

However, Tolkien did not have a great deal of time for the Arthurian tradition, which by his standards was almost modern, insofar as it is largely a conflation of Frankish and Norman 12th century ideas of chivalry, albeit spiced with Celtic faery mythology filtered through Breton story tellers. Although it should be said that it is via a Middle English version of the birth and death of Arthur that elves first appear upon the scene, in Layamon's *Brut.*

In terms of romantic chivalry Farmer Giles is something of an anti-hero. He acquires the reputation first of a giant killer and then of a dragon slayer entirely by a mixture of accident and misunderstanding. Instead of fighting he comes to an accommodation with the creatures involved, principally through his rural cunning and obstinate bargaining, albeit with a fair mixture of "muddling through" to a successful conclusion. In this he also gets the better of a rapacious king and a decadent knightly class. The story is really a celebration of the middle class yeoman rather than of the aristocratic warrior.

The Little Kingdom has a close approximation to actual physical locations – the area of the Thames Valley and the Rollright Stones in Worcestershire - and breathes a certain air of old England that, whilst it may be as much an idealisation as the Logres of knightly chivalry, nonetheless forms an important strand within the fabric of tradition that has become a part of the cultural heritage of the British Isles, for which Tolkien tried to provide a coherent mythology spun out of his own head, distilled from the study of Indo-European languages that were his area of expertise.

In the beginning was the word. From words are spun the stories. From the stories spring self knowledge. As Tolkien's success as a writer seems to demonstrate, from genesis to revelation.

Index

Index

Index

About this Series:

"The Magical Worlds" series, of which the present volume is the first, focuses on the works of renowned literary figures. The first four volumes deal with the group known as "The Inklings." This coterie of influential authors consisted of J.R.R.Tolkien, C.S.Lewis, Owen Barfield, and Charles Williams. Each volume examines one of these authors from the viewpoint of Knight's valuable experience and insight into the realm of the creative imagination and its relationship to the magical powers of the human soul.

Owen Barfield, writing of the manuscript from which these volumes developed, had this to say: *"Because of the combination of information, understanding and insight on which it is founded, [the work] is more than outstanding. It is not in the same league with anything else I have come across."*